I0834063

CITY HALL OF CHINATOWN.

NEW YORK'S

CHINATOWN

AN HISTORICAL PRESENTATION OF ITS PEOPLE AND PLACES.

BY

LOUIS J. BECK.

"The Chinese are here by the order of Providence, the principles of the Declaration of Independence, and the provisions of treaty, and here they are sure to stay until better reasons for their expulsion can be shown than any which have yet appeared."—*M. C. Briggs*, of California.

FULLY ILLUSTRATED FROM LIFE.

NEW YORK:
BOHEMIA PUBLISHING COMPANY,
121 PULITZER BUILDING.

ILLUSTRATIONS.

Chinatown's City Hall	FRONTISPIECE
Map of Chinatown	PAGE 5
Summons to Chong Wah Gong Shaw	14
Interior of a Store	27
Swanpan or Abacus	31
A Domestic Scene	37
In a Second Class Restaurant	48
Scene in a Laundry	59
A Chinese Band	66
Pig Roasting Oven	71
An Actor and His Family	73
Chinese Barber at Work	81
Barber's Outfit	84
Products of Chinese Garden	89
Fan-Tan Players and Utensils	99
A Lottery Ticket	102
Big and Small Footed Women	109
A Slave Girl	111
A Celestial Beauty.	117
Chief of the Low Gui Gow	119
Initiating a Highbinder	131
An Opium Smoking Lay-out	148
Scene in a Chinatown "Joint"	157
Scene in a West Forty-sixth Street "Joint"	171
Smoking a Water Pipe	177
Curious Tobacco Pipes	179
A Registered Laborer	205
In the Joss House	211
"Shall I Buy the Laundry?"	217
A Chinese Funeral	223
A Scene in Evergreen Cemetery	227

PORTRAITS.

	PAGE.
The Author	xii.
Leung Ding Shin	75
Lo Ping and Jo Sung	76
Kwong and Loong	79
Patrolman Michael Kehoe	189
Jung Lee—A Registered Laborer	205
Moy Jin Kee	235
George Appo	251
Chu Fong	263
Mrs. Chu Fong	265
Dr. Jin Fuey Moy	267
Dek Foon	270
Chin You	271
Sue Chung Chew and Family	273
Mrs. Lumina Chew	274
Chin Sing	276
Mrs. Thom Jock and Children	277
Mrs. Mon Lee and Child	278
Mon Ngee	279
Madame Luk Por	280
Dang Fey	282
Chu Jin	283
Charley Tong Sing	285
Yan Phou Lee	287
Lucien Adkins	295
Wm. E. S. Fales	298
Elbert Rappleye	302
Wm. W Young	307
Isaac D. White	312
Horatio Jennings Ward	316
Ed. E. Pidgeon	319
Police Inspector Brooks	323
Moses H. Grossman	330

CONTENTS.

CHAPTER I.

NEW YORK'S CHINATOWN—Its location, origin and development—The first Chinese immigrant and the pioneer mercantile establishment—Number of Chinese now resident in Chinatown and throughout Greater New York . 7

CHAPTER II.

CHINATOWN AND ITS GOVERNMENT—An authority more respected by the Chinese than the legally constituted city government—Its organization and how it exercises its assumed powers 13

CHAPTER III.

CHINATOWN AS IT IS—A run through its streets and a peep into its dark corners—The varied occupations of its people 23

CHAPTER IV.

DOMESTIC LIFE—The wife is always kept in seclusion—Her inferiority in all things—Birth of a child and its treatment—The married people of Chinatown—Some are married by proxy. 33

CHAPTER V.

WITHOUT HOMES—The great body of Celestial immigrants are single men—How they live—The gaudy restaurants of Chinatown—Their bills of fare—Some cookery recipes 45

CHAPTER VI.

CHINESE LAUNDRYMEN—Their organization and strict union regulations—Prices fixed by the unions, and discipline of those who cut rates—What the laundries are and how they are conducted 57

CHAPTER VII.

PECULIAR INDUSTRIES—The many vocations of Chinatown—Their variance from American methods and ideas—The good and the bad inextricably mixed—The useful and the superstitious alike recognized as legitimate and proper 63

CHAPTER VIII.

TONSORIAL ARTISTS—A necessary calling among the Chinese—Universality of head shaving—How the barbers work—The peculiar tools they use—Prices charged . 80

CHAPTER IX.

TILLERS OF THE SOIL—The "Farmers" who provide Chinatown with its peculiar vegetables—Where they work and how they live—An industrious body of Mongolians . 85

CHAPTER X.

CHINESE THEATRE—The only pleasure resort of Chinatown—Singularities of the Chinese drama—The company now occupying the boards there 91

CHAPTER XI.

CHINESE GAMBLING—The passion of the Celestials for games of chance—Descriptions of some of their games—Fan-tan—Lotteries—The Riddle Game—They are all "officially" recognized 95

CHAPTER XII.

PROSTITUTION—Traffic in Chinese women—The dens of infamy of Chinatown—The depth of degradation—The Low Gui Gow 107

CHAPTER XIII.

HIP SING TONG—Organization of the villains of Chinatown—Professional blackmailers, dealers in female slaves and protectors of crime 122

CHAPTER XIV.

OTHER CHINESE SOCIETIES—Fondness for organizations illustrated—Some typical minor associations . 134

CHAPTER XV.

THE OPIUM VICE—Its introduction and spread in New York—Chinamen not the only users of opium, nor Chinatown the only locality where it is used—What the drug is, its use and effects 138

CHAPTER XVI.

OPIUM SMOKING—"Hitting the pipe"—The vice as practiced in Chinatown—How the drug is smoked, and the places where the habit may be indulged—The "Lay-out" described 146

CHAPTER XVII.

IN AN OPIUM DEN—Scenes and observations within a joint in Chinatown as related by a visitor—The average of the dens of vice in that locality 153

CHAPTER XVIII.

A TENDERLOIN JOINT—Where "Mellican" men and women practice the vice—More pretentious apartments, but the same wretchedness—Gamblers and thieves, women and boys mixed together like bait in a box . 167

CHAPTER XIX.

TOBACCO SMOKING—The Chinese are inveterate smokers of the weed—The queer pipes they use—They smoke but little at a time, but often 176

CHAPTER XX.

JOHN BEFORE THE CAMERA—His suspicious nature displayed—Striking a bargain—Humorous incidents illustrative of his character 181

CHAPTER XXI.

SUNDRY OBSERVATIONS—Business integrity of the Chinese—Official testimony regarding them—Less crime in Chinatown than when it was not one quarter so populous—Chinese oaths—Manner of administering them . 186

CHAPTER XXII.

THE CHINESE NEW YEAR—The great festival of the year—The time for settling accounts and beginning anew—Observance of the occasion—Its continuance for twenty days 192

CHAPTER XXIII.

CHINESE CITIZENSHIP—Can a Chinaman become an American citizen?—The question often asked, but not understood—Naturalization of the Mongolians . . 197

CHAPTER XXIV.

THROUGH CLOSED DOORS—Origin of the hostility to Chinese immigration—Efforts of Congress to debar Chinese from the country—How the law is evaded . . 201

CHAPTER XXV.

CHINESE WORSHIP—The religions of the Orient—Confucianism, Buddhism and Taouism—The worship of Joss a fraud, not a form of religion—Some of its repulsive features 207

CHAPTER XXVI.

RESTLESS BONES—An illustration of Chinese superstition —Why the remains of dead Chinamen must be returned to the Celestial empire—How the work of their recovery and shipment is performed 221

CHAPTER XXVII.

MISSIONARY WORK AMONG THE CHINESE—Efforts made to convert the heathen to Christianity—Various missions established among them—What is being accomplished in this direction 230

CHAPTER XXVIII.

GEORGE APPO—BORN TO CRIME—The son of a murderer, after spending half his life in prison follows in the footsteps of his father to a cell for the insane . . 250

CHAPTER XXIX.

TYPICAL CHINESE—Brief sketches of representative residents of Chinatown, male and female, young and old, honest and otherwise 262

APPENDIX.

EXPERT OPINIONS—Views of some of those most familiar with Chinatown and its people 291

PREFACE.

The presence of Chinese in the United States has been a fruitful topic of angry political discussion, of legislative investigation, of congressional legislation and of judicial inquiry for twenty years past. But still they remain with us, and apparently continue to flow in upon us. Why they should come to this country, or why they should not come, are still open questions. To aid in the solution of the vexed problem is the chief purpose of this book. Its aim is to portray the everyday life of those Chinamen who have made the heart of New York City their home—their business occupations, social habits, amusements, religious observances and whatever else is peculiar to them as a race; drawing the pictures from actual life, uninfluenced by favor or prejudice; exaggerating in no particular; concealing no faults; omitting no feature of profitable study; to the end that the reader will be enabled to reach a fair and just conclusion on the questions involved.

That there is the most radical difference between the civilization of the Orient and that of Western nations needs no affirmation. It is manifest at a glance. These people have been born and educated under that form of civilization which has prevailed in the Chinese empire for thousands of years. Our civilization is the outgrowth of a few centuries. Theirs is the most ancient form of any surviving nation on earth; ours the most modern. Here in Chinatown the former is exemplified. It amazes, shocks, startles us. What we esteem criminal is by these people looked upon, if not as being meritorious, at least as innocent. Thus they buy their wives and treat them as drudges. But so did their ancestors from time immemorial; therefore, they ask you, how can it be wrong? They gamble, but gambling is sanctioned by the laws of their native land, and those laws are more venerable than ours which forbid such practices; therefore, how can they be inferior? They smoke opium; but so do other people; then why blame them alone? Moreover, the opium was forced upon them by the leading nation of the West against their most earnest protest, and why should they now be held responsible for the evil it produces?

For the rest, it will be found that these Chinamen are a frugal, industrious, docile, honest class of people, practicing many virtues which should commend them and which might be well emulated by their detractors.

There is one feature of life in Chinatown which cannot fail to attract the attention of every reader. It will be observed that every trade, profession or calling, however exalted or lowly, is governed by a union of its own members. With them the trades union idea is carried to a greater or more perfect extent than with us. With us these unions are only open to the elect—those who may be admitted by the suffrages of those who are already members. With the Chinese any man pursuing a particular vocation may join his union by paying the initiation fee. There is no power to keep him out. And as these unions assume to regulate absolutely the affairs of their particular guilds, the superiority in the matter of fairness and justice of their system over the unions the whites maintain will be manifest. Nor is this the only instance in which western civilization can profit by a study of Oriental customs. No Chinaman can sell out his business, pocket the proceeds, clear out and leave his creditors in the lurch. Through their union system this is rendered absolutely impossible, and every Chinaman must pay his debts.

But we need not enlarge here on these peculiarities. Read the book and be instructed; and then determine if these Chinamen are wholly objectionable and undesirable residents.

In giving this volume to the public the author lays no claim to literary excellence, and merely assumes to portray the habits, manners and customs of the Chinese race in the queer quarter they inhabit and as he has there found them; existing in the very center of the great city of New York, a small Chinese empire, with subjects of this dominion scattered all over its suburbs by the thousands, all of whom give allegiance to the central authority which resides in Chinatown, to which they repair for business or pleasure at short intervals. The language of these people is incomprehensible. Their dress excites curiosity. Their religion is a mystery. Their morals are questionable, viewed by our code. Their pursuits are various; their amusements novel. These interesting things are all described in this work. The merchant will be seen here as in his store; the gambler in his den; the devotee of opium enjoying his deadly pipe; the devout ones kneeling before their "Joss;" the soulless parent selling his offspring to social slavery; the plodding farmer at work in his field; the reckless highbinder trafficking in the worst of crimes; the pedler, the jeweler, the barber, the artist, the doctor, the fortune teller, and all other trades and craftsmen at their several vocations. Their manner of working and style of living are here portrayed, with their mode of preparing the peculiar food in which they delight. The aim has been to give a panorama of living pictures illustrative of the daily life of these strange people who inhabit this queer Chinatown and make it doubly interesting to Americans by reason of the ever recurring hodge-podge of virtue and vice, industry and idleness, prosperity and squalor, honor and shame, which make the locality and its inhabitants so much a mystery and curiosity—rather than a serial romance of questionable veracity.

Above all it has been the aim of the writer to present the Chinaman and his "Chinatown" as they are seen through the glass of the news gatherer in that quaint section of the great Metropolis.

New York, May, 1898.

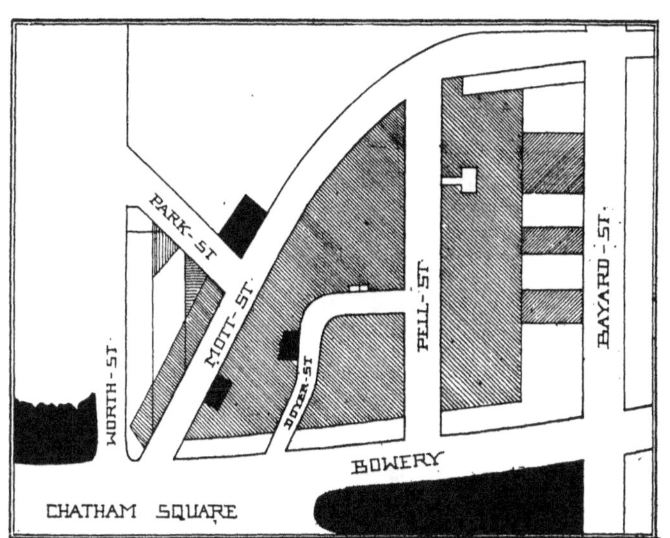

NEW YORK'S CHINATOWN.

CHAPTER I.

NEW YORK'S CHINATOWN.

ITS LOCATION, ORIGIN AND DEVELOPMENT—THE FIRST CHINESE IMMIGRANT AND THE PIONEER MERCANTILE ESTABLISHMENT—NUMBER OF CHINESE NOW RESIDENT IN CHINATOWN AND THROUGHOUT GREATER NEW YORK.

RIENTAL life, its manners, customs, business pursuits, social relations and the everyday intercourse of those so widely differing from us in all respects as do the Chinese, is ever an interesting study to the intelligent American. New Yorkers have the opportunity of observing all this without the necessity of travelling to the Antipodes. China and the Chinese are brought to this great cosmopolitan center for their investigation and study.

The Chinese differ so essentially from the people of the Western world in all respects—in language no more than in dress—business occupations, social relations and general manners of life—in their religion and moral standards; in their extreme clannishness; in the patriarchial system which prevails with them, binding families so close together, and in all the essential features of everyday life—that they naturally, when thrown into strange countries and communities, establish centers where they may congregate and enjoy the pleasures and customs of their native land. There are between 12,000 and 13,000 Chinese in and immediately about New York, a community sufficiently large in itself to populate a good sized town, and quite competent to support the peculiar features of life which prevail in the Flowery Kingdom. Thus a Chinatown has grown up in the very heart of New York City, where Buddha is worshipped and Confucius preached, the morals and manners of the oldest nation in existence are displayed and the civilization of that ancient empire prevails.

The pioneer Chinese resident of New York was Quimbo Appo, a man of great intelligence, gifted with a mind whose keenness startled all white men who came in contact with him. He was born in Chu Fi, in the interior of China, seventy-seven years ago, and fled from his native town to escape punishment for some crime he is said to have committed. He landed in California in 1844; went into the tea business; made considerable money and suddenly disappeared. It became known afterwards that he had sailed as a cook on the United States Ship "Valencia," which brought him to this city.

Upon arriving in New York Appo entered the tea trade again, and soon had established a profitable business for himself. He was a man of interesting personality and made many friends. Those who associated with him were charmed with his winning manner, and there was no greater pleasure in those days, when Chinamen were still but rarely seen on our streets, than to meet Quimbo Appo in a genial mood and listen to the endless stories he had to relate. He drank, however, and Quimbo Appo drunk was a veritable Caliban, dead to all human emotions. At such times he was transformed into a fiend, with an insatiable craving for blood. Woe to the man who crossed the path of Quimbo Appo drunk.

Unfortunately nothing is known in this country of his parents. Whether his moral deformity was a heritage from his ancestors, or merely a spontaneous, accidental tendency to crime, it is impossible to say. There were, however, two Quimbo Appos—or rather a Jekyl and Hyde Appo—one the shrewd, entertaining merchant, full of interesting reminiscences, bright eyed and smiling; the other an inhuman monster, delighting in the worst of crimes.

Quimbo Appo married a woman of the slums, and, in a fit of rage, cut her throat. For this he was sentenced to be hanged, but, by pleading justification for his act, and by allowing himself to be converted to "Tombs Christianity," as the prison conversions are called, he succeeded in obtaining a new trial. He was convicted of murder in the second degree and sentenced to ten years' imprisonment. In 1863 he was pardoned, through the influence of his Christian friends.

He returned to his old life a trifle shabbier and more careless, but in most respects the same old Quimbo Appo. Within a year he quarrelled with a Pole and killed him. For this he served five years in prison. Upon his release he married again.

His second wife was an Irish woman whose name is remembered only as "Cork Mag." The couple had many traits in common. Like her husband the woman was exceedingly agreeable in her sober moments, but under the influence of liquor, lost all control of herself. Many stories are told in Doyers Street of how "Cork Mag" stole all her husband's money and distributed it among several families that were on the verge of starvation. For that she was thrown headlong down a flight of stairs by her liege lord.

One day they were both drunk. They met in the kitchen and after a few words "Mag" threw her husband upon a hot stove. Crazed with pain and rage, he drew from his pocket a keen knife and thrust it, clear to the hilt, into the woman's body. She survived the terrible wound and Appo served a year imprisonment for inflicting it. Of this union George Appo was born.

In 1875 Quimbo Appo was sentenced to seven years' imprisonment for manslaughter in the second degree for the killing of Mrs. Fletcher, a neighbor. After serving three years his mind gave way and the prison physicians declared him to be hopelessly insane. He was transferred to the State Hospital for the Criminal Insane at Matteawan, and there he lives to this day, seemingly forgotten by all the world.

He is an old man now, and the residents of Chinatown would probably not recognize him; but, as a matter of fact, he has not changed very much. To all appearances he is perfectly rational, and for hours he will entertain you with stories of the old days in China and California. He speaks excellent English, and in his sane moments impresses you as being a thorough man of the world. But—bad as he is—and this is pitiful—when the Albany night boat passes Matteawan Appo points to the big search light that flashes in her bow and says proudly:

"That is my diamond. They bring it to me every night."

His delusion is that he is a thousand years old, and upon this matter he will talk seriously for hours. When he is in bad temper they have to confine him in a cell.

Such is Quimbo Appo. He will not live much longer and he will never recover his reason.

The second Chinaman who came to New York and remained was a sailor named Lou Hoy Sing, who left his ship in this harbor in 1862 and took up his residence in Cherry Street. Finding himself lonesome in a great community, he gave himself to the study of the art of love, and soon became so proficient that before the year was ended he captured the heart of an Irish maiden and married her. They lived happily together, contributing two sons to the city's population. One of them later became a policeman, and the other an industrious truckman. Lou Hoy Sing is still living and in good health at the age of 78.

Wo Kee was the title of the first purely Chinese mercantile establishment in the city, which opened about twenty years ago in Oliver near Cherry Street. About it naturally gathered the few Chinese then in the city. The store was moved soon afterwards to Park Street, the growing colony following it. Park Street gave it shelter but a short time, and then it was moved to 8 Mott Street where it still remains, the center, as it was the foundation, of the Chinatown of to-day.

The lower end of Mott Street very quickly filled with Chinese, its former white tenants giving way to the new comers. Gradually the colony increased and spread into Doyers Street, until now the entire triangular space bounded by Mott, Pell and Doyers Streets and Chatham

Square is given to the exclusive occupancy of these Orientals, and they are fast acquiring possession of Bayard Street. This territory furnishes within its borders shelter for 4,000 yellow-skinned traders, artisans, gamblers, amusement caterers and prostitutes, who minister to the wants and entertainment of the 13,000 of their more industrious countrymen who are scattered throughout the metropolitan area. Here the Chinese language is spoken exclusively. Here all manner of Chinese goods, wares and merchandise generally are exposed for sale. Theatre, Joss Houses and restaurants conducted in Chinese fashion are found here. Gamblers and prostitutes abound, inviting the patronage of the industrious, who labor elsewhere, but resort to this center at night and on holidays for their amusements or to transact business. Here the laundrymen from Brooklyn or Jersey or other suburban localities within a radius of fifty miles, meet their "cousins" from Harlem or Hoboken for recreation or business. And here also resides all the authority these peculiar people recognize, and to which they bow with unquestioning obedience.

CHAPTER II.

CHINATOWN AND ITS GOVERNMENT.

AN AUTHORITY MORE RESPECTED BY THE CHINESE THAN THE LEGALLY CONSTITUTED CITY GOVERNMENT—ITS ORGANIZATION AND HOW IT EXERCISES ITS ASSUMED POWERS.

CHINATOWN has a mayor—an officer not recognized by the laws of the land—but still more absolute in his usurped authority and more respected by his fellow countrymen than is the actual chief magistrate of the city of New York. The present incumbent of the office is Ng Shung. He succeeded Chung Yuk Chin and was chosen on Sunday night, April 3, 1898.

This deference is paid to the mayor of Chinatown by all Chinamen, whether resident in the immediate locality or elsewhere, and his authority extends throughout the circuit of thirty miles or more from the Mott Street Temple. Not one in a hundred of the Chinese people have any voice in the selection of this "Mayor." Though an elective officer, the electorate is confined to the leading merchants of Mott, Pell and Doyers Streets, who arrogate to themselves the right to make laws and regulations governing the entire Chinese community in all its ramifications, though, of course, subject to the general municipal laws, theoretically if not practically. Nor is this electorate body elective. It is called Chong Wah Gong Shaw, but has no roll of members nor any expressed title of membership. It has no by-laws or plan of organization. It is a sort of free and easy gathering of the merchants, who pay an initiation fee of $10, and afterward contribute to the common fund as may be needed and as they can severally afford, for the privilege or honor of participating in its deliberations. When for any reason a meeting is desired the mayor issues a number of bottle-shaped pieces of card board, the upper, or head portion, red, and the lower yellow, which the sexton or janitor of the Joss House distributes.

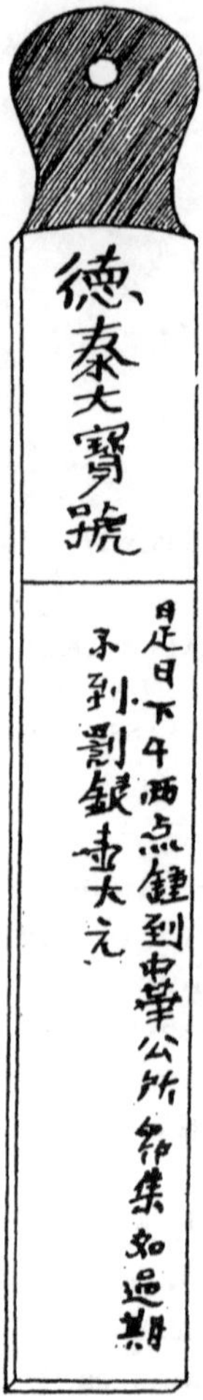

SUMMONS TO CHONG WAH GONG SHAW.

These notices contain the name of the member, the time of meeting and an intimation that a fine of $1.00 will be imposed for failure to attend. At the time of meeting these notices are returned to the sexton and serve as certificates of attendance. Those who assemble in response to the call or invitation proceed to business without roll call or other ceremony, and usually without any show of order. All talk at once; and when the confusion reaches a point only short of a riot the mayor announces a result, to which all submit without question. In the vernacular, "what the mayor says goes," and is a law for Chinamen as binding as that of the ancient Medes and Persians.

In the selection of a mayor the practice is substantially the same. The incumbent's term expiring, or a vacancy in the office occurring, the Chong Wah Gong Shaw is assembled, and those present proceed to nominate their several candidates. Each candidate will probably have a number of supporters. Then ensues a generally disorderly discussion of the merits and fitness of the several candidates, everybody present talking at once, seemingly seeking to drown the voices of the others with superiority of lung power. The wrangling goes on for hours, and usually until all are well tired out with the physical exertion put forth, when the candidate of the longest-winded and most noisy is declared elected, and the exhausted ones submit without protest. No ballot is ever taken. It is a mere contest of brute force and endurance, and the successful candidate so chosen enters upon the duties of his office without let or hindrance from any quarter.

The mayor thus chosen, and the Chong Wah Gong Shaw thus queerly composed, exercise absolute authority over Chinatown not only, but over the entire Chinese population of the metropolitan district. Of course both they and their submissive people are subject to the laws of the city and state; but of those laws the people themselves know but little or nothing, and care less. When apprehended for any violation of them they submit to the judgments imposed with stolid indifference, accepting any punishment that may be meted out to them with that fatalistic philosophy which is a part of their education and religion, and characteristic of their race. But the decrees of the Chong Wah Gong Shaw are promptly made known to them all and command immediate and universal respect.

Every new law or regulation adopted by this queer authority is at once placarded on the official bulletin board in front of the Joss House, which is daily studied by all comers. Whatever is put upon Chinatown's official bill board goes, unless rescinded by a counter notice in similar manner alongside of it.

This official bulletin board is a great institution. It answers the purpose of a published official organ or City Record. As it is kept under the official eye of the sexton or janitor no unauthorized notice can find place upon it. But all the regulations of the Chong Wah Gong Shaw and of the mayor are hereon published and command the attention of the entire community. That publication is "official," and the regulation so posted must be respected and obeyed. Besides these official notices the bill board carries others of a private nature, as the sale or purchase of a laundry or other similar business concern, transfers of chattels, property for sale, men seeking business engagements, and similar advertisements, all written in Chinese characters, and of course unintelligible to the American visitor. Here is a single illustration of the character of the advertisements which find place upon it. It is the announcement of a reformed highbinder, or one who assumes that character. The notice, somewhat freely translated, runs as follows:

"I give notice that I am no longer a member of the Hip Sing Tong. I was hypnotized and fooled and taught to blackmail by that society, but now wish to retain the good will and confidence of the Chinese public.

Quong Len, Petitioner."

All bulletins placed upon this board are supposed to be authorized by the mayor, but any individual can post a notice that is of any interest to the Chinese people.

An important feature of the business committed to the Chong Wah Gong Shaw is the maintenance of a Joss House and the proper use of it by the devotees of idolatry. For "church" and state go hand in hand with these fellows. Though they gamble on the slightest provocation, sell their offspring into prostitution, maintain a large colony of dissolute women, and practice all manner of vice, they are strictly devout in their allegiance to the peculiar forms of belief they profess. Thus the Joss House must be maintained and kept open for the devotions of all comers.

Next in order of importance the Chong Wah Gong Shaw is charged with the duty of seeing that the bones of all dead Chinamen who have been buried six or more years are sent back to the nearest relatives in the town from whence they came. To all Chinamen the Flowery Kingdom is the gateway to Paradise. Through its portals alone can access be had to a happy and peaceful hereafter. No Chinaman will, therefore, leave his native land unless assured that, should he die while abroad, his bones will be returned for final burial in the sacred soil of the land of his birth; and thus it becomes a sacred duty with those residing in any part of the world to see to it that the remains of any of their fellow countrymen who may from any cause, natural or otherwise, be overtaken by death while with them, are sent home for burial. Otherwise the poor fellow's spirit is supposed to be doomed to wander, troubled, anxious and without rest, throughout the ages of eternity. And herein lies the secret of the Chong Wah Gong Shaw's power over the thousands of ignorant and superstitious people who so submissively yield to its authority. If one of their number should be convicted before the Chinatown mayor of an offense against any of the laws or regulations of the governing society, and the mayor should sentence him to a forfeiture of his right to have his remains sent home for burial, the culprit really believes that he is doomed to be an outcast devil in the world of the future.

Another considerable occupation of the Chong Wah Gong Shaw is the settlement of disputes and accounts between Chinamen. It is a court of both civil and criminal jurisdiction, and both nisi prius, appellate and final in its authority. Disputed accounts are laid before the mayor for adjustment. The mayor, if the matter is of any importance, summonses the Chong Wah Gong Shaw to hear the matter. The usual noisy wrangle occurs, pending which the mayor announces a result to which all submit, and the "court" adjourns. Nobody ever assumes to question the absolute correctness of the judgment thus rendered, and as there is no appeal from it "kicking" would be useless. Indeed, should anyone question the decision or presume to refuse submission to it, he would simply be served with a written document, signed by the mayor, forbidding the return of his bones to China in case of death, and that settles it at once. No further resistance is ever offered.

The regulation of fan-tan is another of the functions of the Chong Wah Gong Shaw. Of this interesting game a full account is given in another chapter. Almost every Chinaman is a natural gambler, and fan-tan is the great national game. Hence it is universally played in Chinatown, and though interdicted by American laws and municipal ordinances of this city, it is fully recognized by the law-makers of Chinatown and duly regulated by them in all its details. It also yields a revenue to the mayor, which is scrupulously gathered.

From the foregoing something of the general authority and great power exercised by the Mayor of Chinatown and the Chong Wah Gong Shaw may be inferred. It is wholly unauthorized power, not in any manner recognized by the duly constituted authorities of the city, and has no legal status under American or any other law. Yet it is absolute in its sway and commands the respect and obedience of every Celestial resident, even though no regard ever be paid to American laws or the ordinances of the municipality.

It is an infusion of barbarism into the very heart of this great city which boasts its modern civilization. It regulates business affairs, religion, gambling, prostitution, labor and all other interests of these queer people, and rules them with a tyrant's hand. All complaints of Chinese people to their Consul in this city, the Chinese minister at Washington or even to the Imperial government at Pekin are made through this society, which thus has full recognition by the highest Chinese authority.

The mayor of Chinatown is elected annually in March, the term lasting but one year. Civil service regulations are appplied to this office, though not in a competitive form. But no one is qualified for the office who is not familiar with Chinese literature; has faith in Joss, is obedient to the teachings of Confucius; is an adept at counting, and is possessed of fluency of speech. By tacit understanding the mayor is ineligible for a second term, though there is no law or regulation to that effect. Yet it remains that in the whole history of this queer organization no mayor has ever been re-elected, and the leading Chinamen assert that no one ever will be. This is probably due to the intense jealousy which is a leading element in the Chinese character. The salary of the mayor is $1,000. His office is in the Chong Wah Gong Shaw's building, otherwise the Joss House, at 16 Mott Street. He collects all dues and voluntary contributions, which amount to about $150 a month; the regular income from dues and other sources of the Chong Wah Gong Shaw, about $325 a month; the rentals of the Chong Wah Gong Shaw's property, $175 a month, and the tax on worshippers at the Joss House—50 cents for each devotional visit—which amounts to about $1,000 a year. Thus the total income of the mayor's office is between $8,000 and $9,000 a year.

The mayor's office or chamber is in the rear of the top floor of the building, and is fitted up and furnished in true Oriental style, the furniture and ornamentation being all of Celestial design and manufacture.

The municipal officiary of Chinatown is completed with the sexton or janitor of the temple, Joss House or Chong Wah Gong Shaw's building at 16 Mott Street. This is a position of considerable importance and authority, the incumbent being the mayor's right hand man and executive officer. He serves all papers sent out by the mayor; collects all money due and not voluntarily paid in, and has charge of the building. The position is let annually at public auction, or on proposals, to the highest bidder, usually yielding about $800. That is, the successful bidder pays that amount for the privilege of discharging the duties of the office. He gets his remuneration from fees he is permitted to exact from the worshippers at the shrine of Joss. These fees are fixed by the Chong Wah Gong Shaw. Each worshipper is required to pay fifty cents for offering incense. This is furnished by the janitor and costs but two or three cents for the quantity used by the worshipper. Then he is allowed to exact a fee of twenty-five cents for explaining the text of the prayer turned out by the praying machine. The income from these sources easily runs up into thousands of dollars, making the position lucrative, notwithstanding the $800 paid for it.

The headquarters of Chinatown, as already noticed, is at 16 Mott Street, in the building variously known as the "Chinatown Temple," the "Joss House," the Chong Wah Gong Shaw Building, and derisively called the "Chinatown City Hall." The basement of this building is rented to the Fan-tan Syndicate, and is used as headquarters, and the game is also played there when the observation of the city police can be avoided. The first floor is occupied as a mercantile establishment by the Quong Ying Lung Company. The second floor is used as a restaurant, and is one of the largest in Chinatown. On the third floor is the meeting room of the Mee Shing Gong Shaw, where also every Sunday afternoon at 5 o'clock a Confucian missionary holds forth, as elsewhere mentioned, expounding the tenets of that philosophy and exhorting his hearers to perseverance in the faith. The rear rooms of this floor are occupied by the Chinese Laundrymen's Union. The mayor has his office in the rear apartments of the top or fourth floor. The front of that floor is devoted to the worship of Joss. The particular Joss here enshrined is known as Quan Kong, who is recognized as the god of Chinatown. More familiarly he is called Duke Quan. Quan was supposed to be a man of great strength, like the Hebrew Sampson. Quan is the surname of a particular Chinese family, yet every family worships and honors his effigy as here installed, because, traditionally, he was a man of the greatest physical development and strength. The worshippers believe that this god is able to bestow upon them a portion of his great physical powers. It is the only hall of worship in Chinatown open to the general public.

CHAPTER III.

CHINATOWN AS IT IS.

A RUN THROUGH ITS STREETS AND A PEEP INTO ITS DARK CORNERS—THE VARIED OCCUPATIONS OF ITS PEOPLE.

EV. OTIS GIBSON, the well-known missionary, formerly stationed in China but who for the past twenty years or more has labored among the Chinese of San Francisco, proving himself the friend and champion of the race, tells of the peculiar odors which characterize Chinese settlements and which is popularly supposed to be due to their use of opium. But all Chinamen do not smoke opium any more than do all Germans drink beer, or all Irishmen whisky. Yet the peculiar odor is ever apparent in the immediate vicinity of a

Chinese residence or a company of those people. Mr. Gibson, who is a good authority on that subject, says:

"All countries have their peculiar smell. The very dogs of a country distinguish, at a great distance, the smell of a foreigner from the smell of a native. The Frenchman smells of garlic; the Irishman smells of whisky and tobacco; the German smells of sourkraut and lager; the American smells of corncake and pork and beans; the Englishman smells of roast beef and 'arf and 'arf. The Chinese smell is a mixture and a puzzle; a marvel and a wonder; a mystery and a disgust; but nevtheless a palpable fact. The smell of opium, raw and cooked and in the process of cooking, mixed with the smell of cigars and tobacco leaves, wet and dry, dried fish and vegetables, and a thousand other indescribable ingredients; all these toned to a certain degree of what might be called a shippy smell, produce a sensation upon the olfactory nerves of the average American, which once experienced will never be forgotten."

This pronounced odor will be apparent to the visitor even before he comes in sight of Chinatown, and will prove a sure guide to that locality. It increases in strength as one approaches, while its offensiveness, if it possesses that characteristic, decreases with its density or greater prevalence, until one is finally in the heart of the locality when it quite ceases to be noticed at all.

Chinatown in New York is merely an acquired or appropriated portion of the city. In China the streets are narrow, without sidewalks, and usually without pavements. The buildings are low, flimsy structures of wood, commonly frail bamboo covered with matting. But in New York the streets were opened and improved and the buildings erected before the advent of the Chinese, and are therefore not dissimilar to those in other portions of the city. But in all other respects the visitor finds himself in a veritable wonderland when he enters the locality. He is struck at first with the great number of Orientals he sees in the streets; their constant moving about; their indifference as to whether they use the sidewalk or the roadway; the almost entire absence of females; the incessant jargon with which his ears are assailed, and the tireless bustle and activity manifested on every hand.

Attention is next attracted to the universal decoration and fantastic painting of the buildings. Banners of various designs; paper lanterns of every imaginable shape, size and color; effigies of all manner of repulsive beasts and reptiles, and signs of indescribable design conveying suggestions which are intelligible only to the Chinaman, cover the fronts of the three and four-story buildings, which are themselves painted in red, green, and yellow, and profusely ornamented with gilt and tinsel. Everything is glitter and show. Gaudiness prevails on every hand. Each building rivals its neighbor in its efforts at display and attractiveness. While this bewildering show rivets your attention at first, you will soon observe that the residents pay no attention whatever to it, nor to you either, but jog along intent on their ordinary business or avocations with perfect unconcern regarding all else, though continually pouring out their native language with tireless energy. Who they are talking to, or who is doing the talking, is alike a mystery to you. They do not move along as do Americans or Europeans, in couples, side by side, but string along one after another, carrying on their conversation with their companions who may be in front or behind, though proximity of companions is not indicated by any turning of the head or looking toward each other. It is all a riddle to the uninitiated observer, suggestive of what must have been the experience when the confusion of tongues occurred at the tower of Babel.

If you are accompanied by one who is capable of translating to you the many signs that adorn the places of business you will be struck by the grandiloquent language invariably employed. Here for instance is a small shop filled with various roots and herbs unknown to the American farmer or druggist, over the door to which is displayed in Chinese characters the words:

"The Temple of Heavenly Harmonies."

It is merely an apothecary's shop, the stock in trade being kept for the healing of the sick.

And in this connection the popularity of this word or idea "harmonies" is as remarkable as its use is general. The dealer in meats announces his business as:

"A Thousand Harmonies."

The barber even announces "Everlasting Harmonies" as the product of his tonsorial skill, while the wholesale merchant deals in "Everlasting Harmony Produce." The name of the firm or company is rarely, if ever, given as composed of individuals. Some supposedly lucky phrase is chosen instead, as in the case of the first mercantile concern established here under the title of "Wo Kee," as already noticed. This is not the name of an individual, but another form of "harmony," as indicated by the word 和 which means harmony.

While the Chinese met in the streets seem to be in perpetual motion and driven by their several occupations, a different impression is created on entering their places of business. Visit one of their more pretentious stores—a wholesale establishment, if you please. Its cleanliness and perfect order will strike you. The merchant and his assistants are perfectly neat and clean in their per-

INTERIOR OF A STORE.

sons and attire. They will also be found polite and well behaved. They manifest no curiosity at your visit, though they will receive you with the utmost courtesy and respect. If you intimate a desire to make purchases you will not be hurried. On the contrary, if a known customer, you will very likely be invited to take a seat, and refreshments—usually tea with probably a cracker or a bit of Chinese pastry; and possibly a cigar—will be offered. There is no semblance of hurry or anxiety to sell. The conversation runs on the state of the weather, the latest war news, the condition of finances or any similar general topic. The real business is brought in as an incident of the call; but then shrewdness and business sagacity will be manifested, though in a cautious and diplomatic way.

The motley throng who inhabit these narrow precincts comprise but a fraction (possibly less than one-fourth) of the Chinese of the Metropolitan district. Yet all alike recognize this as their headquarters and submit to the authority emanating from it. The colony which makes Chinatown proper its permanent dwelling place is all busily occupied in some pursuit that ministers to the comfort, pleasure, or passions of the greater number dependent upon it for those things which are peculiar to the Chinese race. The following classification of the occupations of these thousands of strange dwellers, isolated in this great city, is perfectly accurate though not complete:

Candy makers	3
Apothecaries (Chinese doctors)	50
Doctors (Chinese graduates of American colleges)	2
Cigar makers	75
Laundrymen (within 30-mile radius)	8,000
Operators on sewing machines	30
Manufacturers of clothes wringers and laundry supplies	4
Merchants, traders and clerks	175

Sign painters	4
Artists	7
Interpreters	15
Silver and gold smiths	2
Women of respectable families	40
Women—slaves and prostitutes*	3
Young female slaves	12
Vegetable pedlers	12
Transient residents, agents, officers of various associations, loafers and outlaws	150
Highbinders	450
Gamblers	700
Bakers	3
Restaurant keepers and pastry makers	45
Farmers and vegetable growers	75

The Chinese, while exceedingly clannish, are also as markedly jealous and suspicious of each other. They prefer to trade and deal with their own people, and for this purpose will travel many miles; but when so dealing will haggle over prices and watch with the closest attention the measurements, insisting upon full weight or measure, even to excess, in every instance. Their standard table of weights has a "candareen" for its unit, which is one one-hundredth of a tael. The tael equals in weight one and three-quarters ounces avoirdupois. The table runs as follows:

10 Candareens make	1 Mace.
10 Mace make	1 Tael.
16 Taels make	1 Caddy.
100 Caddies make	1 Pecul.

*Note.—There are but few Chinese prostitutes here, but their places are filled by white women of the most degraded class, hundreds of whom occupy apartments in Chinatown and minister exclusively to the passions of the Chinese.

When a Chinaman goes into a shop to buy anything he is not satisfied with having his purchase weighed out to him on American scales, because he wants good, even overweight. This he thinks he secures when the Chinese instrument is used, which is a sort of beam scale or steelyard. When the customer sees the beam of the scale pointing well upward he fancies that he is securing good weight. But his equally crafty countryman knows what he is about. He understands this grasping disposition of his customer, and has his instrument arranged accordingly. Thus if it purported to mark pounds, when a pound is purchased, its arrangement would send the long arm flying upwards when say but 14½ ounces of goods were placed on the other end. So he can give even overweight, according to his scales, and thus satisfy and please his customer, while really cheating him out of an ounce or more of his purchase. It is but another illustration of the truthfulness of the American poet's apt couplet:

"For ways that are dark and tricks that are vain,
The Heathen Chinee is peculiar."

But for all this the Chinese farmer of Long Island, the laundryman of Hoboken, the pedler of Harlem or the house servant of Brooklyn prefers to go to Chinatown to do his trading, where at the same time he can dispose of any surplus money he may have to spare, which he generally leaves behind him in the gambling shops, or upon the women, and incidentally pay a visit to the Joss House and offer up a prayer to his departed ancestors. And so Chinatown is the Mecca of all Chinamen within reach, and is a hive of industry and money getting.

Whoever has had occasion to visit a Chinese store of any pretentions has not failed to notice the bookkeeper, cashier or other employe deftly toying with a lot of buttons strung on wires in a wooden frame which looks like the following illustration:

SWANPAN, OR ABACUS.

This is commonly called a Chinese counting board, probably because it is never seen in use by other than Chinese. It is called "swanpan" by the Chinese themselves, but it is properly an abacus, a mechanical contrivance used for performing or assisting in arithmetical operations. Its use dates very far back in the musty ages of antiquity, even prior to any records we possess of the Chinese nation. It was invented before the introduction of figures. It only came into use in China in the fourteenth century. The Chinese swanpan pictured above is a modification of the original abacus. It is divided into two compartments, the buttons in the upper compartment representing five times the value of those in the lower section. Unlike Chinese writing, the abacus or swanpan is read from the left to the right as in the English system. Thus in the illustration the position of the buttons represents 123,456,789,000,000. One button pushed up against the middle bar and standing alone represents simply the figure 1. A button pulled down in the upper section to meet it would make the representation 6. Nine is represented by four buttons in the lower section and one above. The Chinese use this contrivance for working out addition, division, subtraction and multiplication, calculating interest and all other mathematical work. They use it very rapidly.

Further observation of this unique colony may better be given in the form of descriptions of the various occupations and pursuits which engage the attention and occupy the time of the earnest, industrious and thrifty ones, and the callings of the vicious and the dissolute. For, as among all communities and people of all nationalities, the evil goes with the good. Some of the more important vocations are noticed in chapters by themselves; but glimpses at a few of the minor pursuits are gathered in one chapter. Before entering upon these industries some glances at the domestic life of this queer people will be more appropriate.

CHAPTER IV.

DOMESTIC LIFE.

THE WIFE IS ALWAYS KEPT IN SECLUSION—HER INFERIORITY IN ALL THINGS—BIRTH OF A CHILD AND ITS TREATMENT—THE MARRIED PEOPLE OF CHINATOWN—SOME ARE MARRIED BY PROXY.

HE great Christian "Apostle to the Gentiles," St. Paul, possibly imbibed some of his ultra anti-female ideas from reading the works of Confucius, whose writings were classical centuries before St. Paul was born. Thus, when the apostle wrote the injunction, "Wives submit yourselves to your husbands as unto the Lord;" and again, "Let your women learn in silence with all subjection," and "Suffer not a woman to teach nor usurp authority over the man," he was but carrying out the Confucian idea of the inferiority of the female sex. The philosophers of China, from Confucius down, have all united in assigning the women an inferior place to man, and the great master himself wrote, "Of all people women are the most difficult to manage. If you are familiar with them they become forward, and if you keep them at a distance they become discontented." Hence it is that the Chinaman has no familiar social intercourse with the other sex, but looks upon and treats her in all respects, as an inferior being. Thus the title of the Chinese husband—Jeung Foo—simply defines him as "lord of the house;" and such he is literally and truly. But it may be remarked that a man who has been accustomed since his youth to perform every little duty with a punctilious regard to the ceremonies proper to it, to regulate every motion of his body by fixed rules, and to consider every breach of the elaborate etiquette which surrounds his daily life, as a stain upon his character, is less likely to be actively cruel and violent than more ceremonious and warlike people; and Chinese wives doubtless benefit by the peaceful tendencies of those observances. Happiness is, after all, a relative term, and they are, as a rule, happy under conditions which are fortunately unknown in Europe or America.

The visitor to Chinatown, seeing only men on the streets and an occasional disreputable looking and acting white woman, might infer that there is no real domestic life in that community. But he would be greatly mistaken. There are scores of Chinamen living there in peaceful and contented relations with families of whom they are proud and fond. But that pride and fondness is not manifested in a manner to be comprehended or appreciated by "outside barbarians." In the first place no virtuous and respectable Chinese woman, whether married or single, is ever permitted to show herself in public. Especially is the wife thus carefully excluded from view, except to those of her own sex; and if she has occasion to visit another woman every precaution must be taken to avoid observation. Usually a closed carriage is employed to convey her, even though the distance be less than a block away. Should she, by any accident or design, show herself to any other male than her husband and sons, if she has any, she is disgraced, and has given her husband grounds for divorce under Chinese custom and law. Indeed, she may not show herself to her husband, even, when others are present. The well-bred Chinaman would consider it scandalous for a "lord" or husband to even speak to his wife in the presence of his friends, though guests at his house. So mindful is the wife of this necessary seclusion—so habituated to it is she as a duty—that she herself studies it and is as careful to avoid being seen as the husband can well be to hide her.

Yet despite all this the wife is the drudge of the household unless the family exchequer and the will of the lord permits of the employment of servants. She is required to procure the water in which her husband performs his ablutions; brush his hat and other garments; clean his shoes, and see that he is in all respects in proper condition for his daily duties. But if she happens to follow him into the hall or passageway to give him an affectionate parting, and a male visitor should suddenly appear, she must hide her face lest the neighbors should call him a dishonored husband. Should she venture to flirt with or even speak to any other man on earth, or commit any unfaithful act, she would be liable to be sold as a common prostitute. She does the family cooking, washing and general housework, and never gets a holiday. Having no outside friends, other than helpless slaves like herself, she has no one to tell her troubles and sorrows to but the family joss. She may contract no bills whatever, the husband alone doing that, as well as tending to the marketing, sending home what may be required to eat, drink or wear. The wife must simply carry out the orders of her lord without questioning. She has no voice in the household matters and is not even permitted to eat her meals with her lord, but when he has finished his repast may regale herself on what he may have left.

This severity of discipline is only relaxed when, by good fortune, the poor woman becomes the mother of a son. Then her condition undergoes a radical change. From being a slave and a mere drudge, a nobody and of no account, she is suddenly elevated to a position of honor and importance. She is honored as the mother of a male child, and becomes important by reason of the responsibility thrust upon her of rearing and training the son and heir. This is a position of very great honor, and henceforth the wife becomes the recipient of deference and respect, which follows her through the remainder of her life. The husband treats her thus because she is the mother of his son—the greatest blessing that can come to a Chinaman—while the son reverences her as a filial duty, the performance of which is carefully instilled into him by his teachers throughout his whole course of education. But the woman is still regarded as too sacred a person for vulgar eyes to gaze upon, though she may now enjoy the society of both husband and sons, and has a measure of happiness that might well be envied by many white women.

But while the Chinese woman is thus rigidly secluded from public observation, and is so commonly a mere drudge, she is often indeed the pet of her lord, who heaps upon her every indulgence and pleasure compatible with Chinese etiquette. He provides her with pretty and attractive clothing and delights in seeing her handsomely dressed. The wife reciprocates this affectionate liberality by studying to make her appearance as attractive as possible. Especially is she careful in the dressing of her

A DOMESTIC SCENE.

hair. In this all Chinese women take peculiar care and pains. It is put up in various forms, usually in broad, flat plaits or braids, arranged in every conceivable form about the head, thickly plastered and stiffened with a kind of bandoline which holds it in shape for several days. The sides are adorned with a plentiful assortment of pins and ornaments. Flowers also are used in profusion when obtainable, or artificial blossoms are substituted when the real cannot be had. Much taste is shown in the colors chosen and the arrangement in these elaborate coiffures.

The Chinese colony of this city embraces 84 married couples or families. Of this number the wives in 36 instances are Chinese women, while 48 of them are white. The white wives may be divided into three classes: 1—Respectable women regularly and formally married to Chinamen, and duly recognized as wives by the Chinese as well as by all others; 2—Women who were formerly prostitutes, but are now married according to Chinese customs to men with whom they live, and who claim and acknowledge them as wives; and 3—Common prostitutes living with some particular man as his common law wife. The last are looked upon more in the light of mistresses than as wives, though several of them have children, though none of them more than two. The total number of children of these mixed marriages is 47, of whom 28 are sons and 19 daughters. The families in which the white wife is counted as of the first class are chiefly Christian families, with whom the offspring is looked upon and treated with equal fairness and affection, whether male or female. The second class wives are mainly ignorant and depraved women who treat their female children very much as do their husbands, being careless and indifferent as to whether they are well or illy treated. Yet possibly in secret they have as much fondness for them as for their boys, but not much for either. The third class of white wives have no appreciation of morality or virtue themselves, and are usually utterly careless regarding their children, whether boys or girls.

There are 30 pure Chinese families—that is, families in which both husband and wife are Chinese. The wives in almost every instance have been purchased, as are nearly all Chinese wives, either here or in China. The couples have been married after the Chinese fashion only, but are duly recognized as regularly married people; and live together as such. Twenty-one of these families have children, the total number of full blooded Chinese children being 32. Of these, 22 are sons and 10 daughters. In all these cases the daughters are looked upon and treated as inferiors, incumbrances, chattels to be disposed of as soon as the time and fitting opportunity arrives. The lower order of these Chinese parents are quite indifferent in disposing of their daughters, whether they are to be made wives or prostitutes. The better classes, however, prefer to sell their offspring for wives, and they generally find no difficulty in doing so because of the scarcity of girls of their nationality in this community who are eligible for wifehood.

When a Chinese male baby is born in Chinatown practically every one knows it. It is talked of in the Joss House, in restaurants and on the street corners. The first morning after the birth of the child the father hastens out to receive the congratulations of his cousins and friends.

On the third day after the child's birth he is washed for the first time. This is an occasion of great moment, and the relations and intimate friends are invited to take part in the ceremony. Each guest is expected to bring with him an onion and some cash—emblems of keen wittedness and wealth—which are formally presented to the child. Water in which scented herbs and leaves have been fused is used in the ablution, and when the process is over all present join in offering sacrifices to the family joss.

When the baby is a month old the parents give a dinner in one of the restaurants, if their residence does not afford the facilities required. At this time a name is given the child, its head is shaven and the queue started to grow. When the child receives its name the friends of the father give an abundance of presents, such as gold bracelets, silks, etc. After the baby is able to walk he may be seen in his father's store or on the street, and is a curiosity, if of no interest, to the customers.

But to return to the male offspring. The day and hour on which he is born are considered as portentious for the future good or evil of the child as can well be conceived. Thus we are told that a child born on the fifth day of a month, and especially on the fifth day of the fifth month, will either commit suicide in after life, or will murder one or the other or both of his parents. A child born at noon is believed to be a sure inheritor of wealth and honor, while he who comes into the world between the hours of nine and eleven will have a hard lot at first, but great wealth later. The unfortunate one who comes into existence between three and five o'clock is doomed to poverty and woe throughout his life. Mr. Dennys, in his "Folklore of China," tells us that the day of birth also exerts influence over the future of the new-born child. Thus we have this rythmical forecast of the future of children born on the several days of the week:

Monday's child is fair of face;
Tuesday's child is full of grace;
Wednesday's child is full of woe;
Thursday's child has far to go;
Friday's child is loving and giving;
Saturday's child works hard for its living;

But the child which is born on Sabbath day,
Is blythe, and bonnie and good and gay.

As they have no Sabbath day in China some doubt is cast upon the authenticity of this entire schedule. But among the Chinese it is certain that the baby who cries long will live to be old, while the one whose weeping is habitually intermittent will have a precarious life at best. Babies whose cries die out, or the tone of whose crying is deep, or who open their own eyes, or who constantly move their hands and feet, are doomed by the physiognomists to early death, while the child who walks, teeths and speaks early has a bad disposition, and will turn out unlovable.

If the baby is a girl the father makes no demonstration of joy at its birth; he gives no dinner, and in fact tries to forget its very existence. She is sold as soon as possible.

Filial piety is the leading principle in Chinese ethics and really lies at the base of whatever religion they practice. Confucius insisted on it most strenuously, and all his disciples down to this day inculcate it. "Filial piety," said Confucius, "consists in obedience according to propriety; in serving one's parents when alive according to propriety; in burying them when dead according to propriety." The "Book of Rites," which is the universal law of China, enjoins, that "during the lifetime of his parents a son should not go abroad, or, if he does, then only to a fixed place. When at home he should rise at the first cock-crow, and having washed and dressed himself carefully, should inquire what the wishes of his parents are as to the food they would eat or drink. He should not enter a room unless invited by his father, nor retire without permission; neither should he speak unless spoken to." These precepts are strictly obeyed by all Chinamen, if not literally to the letter, at least in spirit.

All the foregoing applies mainly to the male offspring. The female child is considered of no account—an incumbrance rather than a blessing. They are commonly sold at the earliest possible day, as well in America as in China. The laws of both countries alike forbid this practice, though under Chinese law it is permitted when effected with the sanction of the child. But that prohibition is practically ignored, just as is the law which forbids infanticide; yet in China it is a common practice, more especially among the poorer classes, to put the girl baby to death as soon as its sex is revealed. This practice is even defended. "What," they say, "is the good of rearing daughters? When they are young they are only an expense; and when they might be able to earn a living, they marry and leave us."

It was brought out in a recent case in one of the courts of this city, by the testimony of a Chinaman who had been arrested for an assault on a five-year-old girl, that the mother of the child, Mrs. Annie Lee, a white woman, the wife of a Chinaman, had sold her daughter to the Chinaman for $44. This was denied by the mother, who said she had simply "given the child to the Chinaman and he was taking good care of her." The Gerry Society took up the case and had the child turned over to its care. Mrs. Lee had one girl by a former husband, a white man named Glackner. This child was the alleged victim of the assault, and is now in St. Ann's Home. She has another daughter of which her Chinese husband is the father, which is alleged to have been sold to a Chinaman as his wife. They live at 43 Mott Street. Two other children are with the mother.

There are a number of Chinamen now living in Chinatown who are looking forward with more or less impatience to the time when they can return home and claim the wives already selected for them by their parents, and to whom they are actually engaged according to the Chinese methods. It being considered a grave breach of etiquette for young men and maidens to associate together, the presumption is that the man never sees his bride until she becomes such by actual marriage. Of course it does occasionally happen that either by stealth or chance a pair become acquainted and mutually agree to an engagement. But whether they have thus associated, or whether they are perfect strangers, the first formal overture must of necessity be made by a "go-between," who, having received a commission from the parents of the young man, proceeds to the house of the lady and makes a formal proposal on behalf of the would-be bridegroom's parents. If the young lady's father approves the proposed alliance, the suitor sends the lady some presents; next the parents exchange documents, which set forth the hour, day, month and year when the young people were born, and the maiden names of their mothers. The price demanded for the girl, if she is being sold, as is usually the case, is also agreed upon and paid over. Astrologers are then called in to consult about her horoscopes and, should these be favorable, the engagement is formally entered into.

Thus it happens that these young men of Chinatown, or the most of them, have never seen their future wives, and can have no conception of their beauty and attractiveness or the reverse, beyond what their parents may have communicated to them. Still they are eager to take the fatal plunge. They want to set up house keeping and provide heirs for the fortunes they are making in this alien land, and who shall reverence and honor them when they shall be dead.

But not all these benedicts are willing to wait the indefinite time that may transpire before they can consider themselves wealthy enough to return to China and claim their wives. Meantime their selected wives are advancing in years and may become tired of waiting; or their parents may weary of feeding them, as rice is not any too plentiful in a thickly populated province like Kwong Tung for instance. Thus it happens that marriages have taken place in China where the lady lives, while the husband is still in Chinatown, New York. Lee Yen Shee, of 11 Mott Street; Wong Sing Wah, of 18 Mott Street; Yip Mon Hong, of 22 Pell Street; Yong Po Yum, of 13 Pell Street, and others who might be named are among the married men who have never seen their wives. They have simply been married by proxy in order to make sure of the chosen one. In such cases the negotiations are conducted in China by the respective parents in the usual way; the documents are exchanged, and the money is paid over to the lady's parents; cards of engagement are circulated and the engagement is perfected in due form. The cousins and friends are invited to the nuptial feast. But when the ceremony is to be performed, in the absence of the bridegroom, a rooster is substituted. A nice healthy rooster is selected and decorated with a red silk banner and gold jewelry. The nearest male relative of the absent groom acts as guardian. He holds the rooster in the performance of the ceremony, meeting the bride while she is coming to the bridegroom's house; worshipping the ancestors before the family joss; bowing to the cousins and friends, and whatever else custom requires of the bridegroom, all the while carefully holding the fowl. When the ceremony is over the bride takes the rooster and must feed him whenever she herself eats. If the rooster should die during the bridegroom's continued absence he is entitled to a decent burial, as if he was the real husband. Should he live until the husband's return the latter will then kill the bird and he will be served up as meat at dinner. On such a slender thread does the matrimonial bliss of many Chinamen hang.

———o———

CHAPTER V.

WITHOUT HOMES.

THE GREAT BODY OF CELESTIAL IMMIGRANTS ARE SINGLE MEN—HOW THEY LIVE—THE GAUDY RESTAURANTS OF CHINATOWN—THEIR BILLS OF FARE—SOME COOKERY RECIPES.

HE large majority of Chinamen who come to this country, quite naturally, are young men, many of them mere boys. They are starting out in life, and come here, as do other immigrants, to make their fortunes. But, unlike other races, they merely remain here after accumulating a living competency. Hence they are mostly unmarried. Of course they have no homes other than the bachelor quarters they may provide for themselves in the vicinities where they labor.

The thousands of laundrymen scattered through the Metropolis—and these constitute by far the largest number of our Chinese population—live in their laundries. Usually they have a back room in which they do their washing, and there also they do their cooking. Their ironing tables furnish them satisfactory beds, or else they sleep in rough bunks made against the wall in the back room. They require but little cooking, being content with an occasional piece of pork boiled, or some stewed fowl. Their main staple is rice, always boiled, and fresh greens of some kind. When this simple regimen palls their appetite a visit to Chinatown affords them opportunity for a change by indulgence in the more elaborate menus provided by the gaudily decorated restaurants of that locality, wherein are served all the peculiar viands and much relished dainties of their native land.

The well-to-do merchant employs a servant who prepares his meals for him in a small back room of his store. But when he has visitors or essays a dinner of ceremony, he invariably resorts to the restaurants. The majority of the dwellers in Chinatown proper provide themselves with sleeping places only in which they do their eating much as do the scattered laundrymen, resorting to the restaurant occasionally. All, however, have the national craving for good living, which can only be satisfied at these establishments. And as most of the Chinamen within a radius of fifty miles visit the great center, if possible, at least once a week, they indulge in as good a meal as they can afford when there. Thus the patronage of the restaurants is ample, and especially so on Sunday, which is the great congregating day, when the locality is fairly thronged with people from all portions of the metropolitan district.

The most gorgeously decorated and illuminated buildings in Chinatown are those occupied by these restaurants. The more pretentious of them usually occupy upper floors in three or four story buildings, having balconies across their fronts, the buildings themselves being gaudily painted in deep green with red and gilt trimmings. Chinese lanterns are suspended in reckless profusion from every available point. The interiors are also decorated in similar Oriental style. The eating rooms are kept with scrupulous cleanness, and no unusual dirt will be found in the kitchens. A recess or alcove off the dining room, furnished with a cot and covered with a portierre is generally provided for the use of those who may wish to indulge in a short nap after dinner. The furniture of the dining rooms is not materially different from that of any other restaurants. Tables are provided for parties of two, four or more, as required. Ordinary chairs are used, and the ware has no peculiarity except in the tea cups, which are provided with two saucers, in one of which the cup stands and the other is used as a cover. This arrangement is rendered necessary because of the peculiar manner in which the tea is served. The dry leaf is placed in the cup, which is then filled with boiling water and covered. When sufficiently steeped it is sipped rather than drank, with neither milk or sugar. When the first infusion is exhausted the cup is refilled with boiling water, which, by leisurely drinking, attains sufficient strength without addition of more tea. Cutlery forms no part of the table furniture, the national chop sticks being supplied instead, though knives and forks will be furnished if specially called for by "Mellican" or other patrons not accustomed to the use of chop sticks. Meats, when served, are cut and carved into suitable mouthful portions before being placed upon the table. The eatables are brought in in a common receptacle—a deep dish or bowl—from which each guest at the table helps himself at pleasure, dipping in his chop sticks and conveying what is taken directly to his mouth.

Other restaurants of a cheaper character abound, commonly occupying basements. They are less lavishly dec-

IN A SECOND-CLASS RESTAURANT.

orated and furnished. Their tables have no linen, but are otherwise as clean as the average cheap American restaurant. The viands provided are not so peculiar and are served with much less pretention. They are patronized by the laboring classes and outlaws, and quite largely by the lower classes of white people who visit

Chinatown for vicious purposes, dissipation or mere curiosity.

There are seven restaurants in Chinatown which rank as first-class places, and four others of the second or lower class, some of which would more properly be called mere eating houses. Those of the first-class are the following: Hon Heong Lau, 11 Mott Street; King Heong Lau, 16 Mott Street; Me Heong Lau, 14 Mott Street; Way Heong Lau, 20 Mott Street; Gui Ye Quan, 34 Pell Street; Mon Li Won, 24 Pell Street, and Kum Sun, 16 Pell Street. The menu and prices charged in these several places are substantially the same. They each serve a variety of dishes classified according to the price charged as per the following

BILL OF FARE.

Two Dollars per Dish:—

Yu Chie—(Shark's Fins).
Wong Ye Tao—(Sturgeon Head).
Yen War—(Bird's Nest).
She Kiao—(Air Bladder of Eels).
Sze Kwa Ap—(Deviled Duck).
Don Bark Gop—(Steamed Squab).
Sut Ye—(Snow Moss).
Shake Ye—(Rock Moss).
Sen Mi—(Angel's Beans).
Hoi Tsam—(Beach de Mare).
Bow Ye—(Holiotis).

Seventy-five Cents per Dish:—

Por Law Gai Pin—(Fried Chicken, Boneless, with Pineapple).
Chow Gai Pin—(Fried Boned Chicken).
Tao Pin—(Fried Pig's Paunches).

Chow You Ye—(Fried Duck's Web).
Park Gop Song—(Fried Minced Squab).
Chow Loong Har—(Fried Lobster with Vegetable).
Chow Foo Kwar Gai—(Fried Chicken with Balsam Pears).
Chow Gai Sue Mean—(Fried Noodles with Boneless Chicken).

Soups—Twenty-five Cents a Dish:—

Sue Kwa Kiang—(Sponge Squash Soup).
Tso You Kiang—(Mushroom Soup).
Chop Suey Kiang—(Giblets and Pork Fried).
Hoy Shum Kiang—(Beach de Mare Soup).
Too Kwar Kiang—(Balsam Pear and Pork Soup).
Ho She Kiang—(Dried Oyster Soup).

Fifty Cents a Dish:—

Chow Mean—(Fried Noodles).
Chow Fune—(Fried Rice and Noodles).
Foo Yong Dan—(Ham and Egg Omelet).

Fifteen Cents a Dish:—

Shen Arp—(Boiled Duck).
Park Chum Gai—(Plain Boiled Chicken).
Ap Hoy Wan Ton—(Stuffed Noodles and Duck's Leg).
Ap Hoy Mean—(Noodles with Duck's Leg).
Chop Suey—(A Hash of Pork, with Celery, Onions, Bean Sprouts, etc.).
Chop Shu—(Broiled Loin of Pork).
Yung Dow Foo—(Stuffed Bean Cheese).
Lo Yok—(Pig's Ears, Snout and Paunches Mixed).
Chow Kai Tsoi—(Fried Green Rapes).

An almost endless variety of cheaper dishes are served, down to a simple bowl of rice for five cents. Then follows—

Miscellaneous, Ten Cents per Order:—

Li Chee Kon—(Dried Li Chee Nuts).

Kon Tau Li Chee—(Preserved Li Chee Nuts).

Faraday Young Tao—(Star Fruit from Faraday).

Wong Pe—(A small fruit of the lemon variety).

Kum Ghet—(Same as above, but larger).

Ching Moi—(Preserved Green Apricots).

Por Law—(Preserved Pineapple).

Sar Lee—(Preserved Pear).

Loong Ngou—(Dragon's Eyes—a fruit similar to Li Chee).

Shup Kwar—(Preserved Citron).

Gai Ngang Go—(A confection made the shape of a chicken's neck).

Pastry, Twelve Cents a Plate or Three Cents Each:—

Gai Don Go—(Sponge Cake, steamed or baked).

Dow Sar Bow—(Bean Jelly Dumpling).

Tom Yok Bow—(Sweetmeat Dumpling).

Chop Shu Bow—(Roast Pork Dumpling).

Park Sung Go—(Fermented Rice Flour Pudding).

You Char Kwai—(Doughnuts).

Wau Shoo—(Dumpling made of Lobster and Vegetables).

Dem Sum—(Minced Pork Dumplings).

Chee Ma Beang—(Cake Flavored with Seaman Seed).

Fook Yok Beang—(Flat Cake Stuffed).

Wan Gaw Go—(A Gummy Cake).

Soo Beang—(Crusted Cake Stuffed).

Ham Chit Soo—(A thin Snap Cake, highly flavored).

Lok Dau Go—(Cake made of Green Bean Flour).

Wines and Liquors, Fifty Cents a Pot; Twenty-five Cents a Cup:—

Moi Kwai Lo—(White Rose Wine).

Ng Kar Pe—(Palm Root Wine).
Park Nor Mi—(White Rice Liquor).
Ching May—(A liquor flavored with fruits).
Sam Pen—(Medical Brandy).

Tea, five cents per cup.

Of restaurants and eating houses of the second class there are four, located as follows: Me Lau Goi, 30 Pell Street; Chay Heong Hen, 13, 17 and 20 Doyers Street. The bills of fare in these places is far more limited and the prices lower. The service, as mentioned already, is vastly inferior and the surroundings anything but desirable. The staple dishes served at these places are usually ready cooked. The prices charged are five and ten cents, according to the demand of the guest.

BILL OF FARE.

Chop Shu—(Roast Pork).
Yok Bang—(Minced Pork).
Chee Kok—(Pig's Feet).
Ngow Park Mum—(Stewed Beef).
Ham Dau—(Salted Eggs).
Lap Chong—(Dry Sausages).
Chay—(Greens).
Loong Ngor Bark—(White Cabbage).
Fan or Arn—(Rice, a Big Bowl).

A bowl of soup is furnished with the foregoing free of charge.

Wine and liquors fifteen to twenty-five cents a pot.

A hen coop will be found adjacent to every restaurant kitchen, amply supplied with live chickens, ducks and pigeons, ready for slaughter and cooking as required. The regulations of the Board of Health in this regard do not seem to bother the Chinaman at all. They must have live birds or none at all; this is the Chinaman's idea of fitness for eating. If it were not for want of room they would keep a pig pen next to their chicken coops.

The menus might be extended with undoubted satisfaction to the Chinese customers by these additions made from a bill conspicuously displayed as a special attraction over the door of a restaurant in Canton, China:

Cat's flesh, one basin.............	10	cents.
Black cat's flesh, one small basin...	5	cents.
Wine, one bottle...............	3	cents.
Wine, one small bottle..........	$1\frac{1}{2}$	cents.
Congee, one basin..............	2	cash.
Ketchup, one basin.............	3	cash.
Black dog's grease, one tael.......	4	cents.
Black cat's eyes, one pair........	4	cents.

The price put upon these delicacies are to be commended, even though the viands themselves be not relished.

The proprietors of the restaurants of Chinatown do not seem to consider that service is any part of their business. Their waiters do not wear white aprons, nor are they ubiquitous and attentive to the wants of guests. They stand near at hand to receive orders, which are bawled out to the cook in the kitchen at the further end of the building, calling for the exercise of no little lung power. Unless you are familiar with the habit you might fancy he was calling to his partners to come and fight you. When served the waiter leaves you.

A word as to the habits and manners of the Chinese customers at the table. They are armed with a pair of chop sticks, which seem to be all that is necessary for them. They scoop the rice from the bowl into their mouths with the sticks, and use the same sticks to take up anything they may fancy from the main dishes.

They are very expert in the use of these awkward utensils, and can pick up anything with them from a chunk as large as an egg to a particle as small as a pin. All ceremonial dinners are given at these restaurants. Merchants here entertain their guests, and are frequently very lavish in their expenditures. At such entertainments, while the same habits of eating prevail, the highest courtesy is maintained in social intercourse, and strict etiquette is observed. On Sundays dinner parties are numerous, and the facilities of the establishments are fully tested. They also do a good business every day, but largely with individual patrons. Their average daily receipts are estimated at $500, $200 of which comes from white customers, $275 from Chinamen, and $25 from negroes, who seem to delight in frequenting the lower class places.

A Chinese cook of the first class employed in these restaurants is paid $80 a month and his board. But he must be an adept at his business, trained to it in China, and thoroughly familiar with all dishes peculiar to the native land. Cooks of the second class receive $60 a month. They may have acquired their trade since coming to this country, but must be proficient in it, and perfectly familiar with Chinese dishes and condiments. Other cooks earn from $33 to $40 a month, which is probably all they are worth. They may never have seen the inside of a kitchen before coming to America, and know but little of the preparation of choice Celestial dishes. But they can fry a piece of pork, boil or stew a chicken, and prepare table greens, and that is about all that is required of them in the cheap restaurants.

The supplies used in these restaurants, other than the plain meats, fowls and fresh vegetables, are all imported from China. The quantity of these imported supplies used is considerable, and adds no little to the revenue of the San Francisco Custom House, through which it is chiefly entered. Every steamship coming from China brings consignments of edibles for these restaurants.

HOW TO COOK RICE.

Rice is the great staple of Chinese consumption, and is even more commonly and generally eaten by them than are potatoes by Americans. Because of its universal use by them the Chinese have become proficient in its prepăration. An expert Chinaman furnishes the following directions for its preparation and cooking:

"In the first place," he says, "care and judgment should always be exercised in the selection of the rice, that it is not too old and hard. New or soft rice is always preferable for cooking. Wash it thoroughly in cold water. It should be washed repeatedly, in fresh water every time, and until the water remains perfectly clear after the washing. Three or four washings are not any too many. The amount of water used in cooking should be sufficient to cover the rice and rise about an inch above it in the cooking vessel. Use cold water always and let it come to the boiling point gradually over a fire of but medium intensity. When it begins to boil thoroughly remove the vessel to the back part of the stove, or where it may be kept steaming for about fifteen minutes, when it will be sufficiently cooked. This will be manifested by its being slightly scorched on the bottom. The vessel used must be provided with a cover which fits perfectly tight. A thick iron pot is the best. Put no salt into the rice or water while cooking. If salt is used while cooking, the grains will swell up in a peculiar form and turn black. The allowance of time for cooking the rice should be forty-five minutes—twenty minutes for it to come to the boiling point, and twenty-five minutes for steaming—according to your judgment."

SEE OW SAUCE.

A popular sauce affected by the Chinese is called See Ow. It is made from beans, star aniseeds and spices, and exposed to the sun. It is very high flavored, and the Chinese epicure thinks that it beats any other condiment on earth.

CHINESE SAUSAGE.

The sausage affected by the Chinese epicure and manufactured by the Celestial artisans is made of fresh pork cut in the shape and size of dice, and not chopped, as in the meat of ordinary sausages. The fat and the lean is used in equal proportions. They are seasoned with Wah Yem, a certain variety of mineral salt found only in the Province of Souchin, China (which costs in Chinatown about 15 cents a pound); a compound composed of China corn brandy and a simple syrup made of rock candy; spice of mandarin; orange peel; Sou Chin pepper; root of the nutmeg tree; star aniseeds and cinnamon. They are colored and finished with bean sauce, stuffed in skins and dried in the sun, to which they are exposed five days. They are then kept in a tightly covered jar for at least five days, when they are ready for eating. They are not fried, but steamed, fifteen minutes being the usual allowance of time for their cooking. They are quite frequently steamed in the same pot with rice. This sausage costs 28 cents a pound. Its flavor is very high and lasting. The writer knew a respectable American lady who married a Chinaman solely to enjoy Chinese sausage with rice.

CHAPTER VI.

CHINESE LAUNDRYMEN.

THEIR ORGANIZATION AND STRICT UNION REGULATIONS—PRICES FIXED BY THE UNIONS, AND DISCIPLINE OF THOSE WHO CUT RATES—WHAT THE LAUNDRIES EARN AND HOW THEY ARE CONDUCTED.

AS THE laundrymen constitute by far the larger portion of the Chinese in and about the Metropolis, they naturally deserve prominent mention. It is true that but few of them are residents of Chinatown proper; but, though scattered over an area of about thirty miles in all directions. from that center, they all recognize that as their headquarters. To Chinatown they repair weekly, or as often as possible, for such supplies as they may need, as well as for social intercourse with their countrymen, or for devotion; pleasure and amusement. To

Chinatown they also look for regulations to which all Chinamen in the vicinity are subject. As there are 8,000 laundrymen in this vicinity they constitute more than fifty per cent. of the entire Chinese population. It is obvious, then, that their patronage goes very far toward supporting the various and peculiar enterprises of the compact central community.

The Chinese washermen recognize, as do all their countrymen in the vicinity of New York, the authority of the Mayor of Chinatown and the Chong Wah Gong Shaw, notwithstanding that they have no voice in the selection of either. But they have organizations of their own which have particular oversight of their calling and in which they do participate as members. They are the Chop Sing Hong and the Sing Me Hong. These are merely unions of the men engaged in the laundry business. The former embraces those employed in the Boroughs of Manhattan and The Bronx and Jersey City only, and the latter those working in the Borough of Brooklyn and Hoboken.

All laundrymen throughout the metropolitan territory are members of one or the other of these unions or hongs. No Chinaman could carry on his business for a single day without affiliation with the hong. All alike are eligible to membership without any ceremony of making application or being voted for. All that is required is the payment of an admission fee of $5 and the subsequent payment of dues, which are fixed at 25 cents per month per man working in any one laundry. Both hongs have their headquarters in Chinatown, and work together in most perfect harmony.

The Chop Sing Hong, or New York Union, has its headquarters at 28 Mott Street. Its officers, who are supposed to be always on duty at headquarters, are a president, secretary and two collectors. These are chosen by the votes of the members, and are paid salaries which are fixed by the hong. The hong fixes the prices which are to be charged by its members for work. These

SCENE IN A LAUNDRY.

are now, for laundrying shirts, 10 cents; undershirts and drawers, 7 cents each; handkerchiefs, 2 cents each; cuffs and collars, 2 cents each; and so on throughout the entire washable wardrobe. The laundryman, it is understood, must charge these prices as a minimum. He may charge as much more as he pleases or can get; but if he charges a penny less, woe betide him. The prosecutors of the hong will be after him quickly and will pursue him relentlessly. If he is not brought to terms by the power and influence of the hong itself or its agents he will be haled before the regular courts of the city, either in a civil action for alleged debt, a criminal prosecution for larceny, or some other fictitious offence, for which abundant evidence will be forthcoming.

The hong also undertakes to protect its members in the monopoly of the territory assigned them. The bounds of each man's district are strictly defined, and no other laundry, conducted by a Chinaman, is permitted to encroach. When a new laundry is set up in doubtful or unassigned territory against the wishes of existing laundries, the hong will send its agents to the intruder to labor with him. If he is a trespasser on another's territory, he will be quickly warned away and made to go. If he is merely a new comer, making one too many for the neighborhood, he will be bought off if possible, or, if he is obdurate, will be driven off by similar methods to those pursued against the cut rate fellow. If he sells out to the hong, then the location is registered by street and number and the hong guarantees neighboring laundrymen from further interference in that locality. In that case these neighboring laundries are assessed the amount it has cost the hong to get the intruder out.

When a laundryman desires to dispose of his business, he must first give notice of the fact by placing an announcement on the bulletin board of his hong, as well as that of the Chong Wah Gong Shaw, giving a full description of the establishment, the name by which it is known, the number and name of the street where located, and the name of the borough, city or township and state.

The purchaser of a laundry must also in a like manner publish the facts, with exact locality, the price to be paid for it, and the terms of payment made or to be made. The buyer has no right to pay more than 10 per cent. of the purchase price to bind the bargain; the remaining 90 per cent. must be paid at the headquarters in Chinatown in the presence of members of the Chong Wah Gong Shaw at the time mentioned in the bulletined notice. This arrangement gives opportunity to all creditors of the retiring laundryman to present their accounts to the mayor for settlement. The seller is only allowed to receive the balance of the money after all his debts so presented have been paid. The hong will not recognize any sale or purçhase not made in strict accordance with this regulation.

The Sing Me Hong, or union, of outside laundrymen is organized on precisely the same principles and is governed by very similar regulations. Its headquarters are at 16 Mott Street. Its members chiefly do business in Brooklyn and throughout the Borough of Queens and in Hoboken, N. J. Its prices are the same as those of the Hop Sing Hong. The hong recognizes the laundry, not the individual, and they cannot be transferred from one to the other, but must continue to pay the monthly dues of 25 cents to the hong to which they belong.

A Chinese laundry is owned and conducted by one or two proprietors. The smaller concerns owned by a single man command business enough merely to keep him at work, with possibly an occasional rush, which he is able to dispose of with the voluntary help of his "cousins" or friends. Where the permanent business exceeds the ability of a single man to dispose of, two proprietors take it, usually contributing equal shares of the capital stock. They work together, eat together, and sleep together, and at the end of the year divide the earnings equally. If the work exceeds the ability of the two proprietors, workmen are hired. The help so employed is paid $8, $10 or $12 a week, according to the amount of work required to be done and the ability of the workman to dispose of it. This ability does not imply mere skill, but more particularly physical strength, rapidity and endurance. In addition to his wages the workman receives his board and lodging as well. Neither the proprietors nor their workmen recognize any limit to a day's work. They work continually until the work in hand is finished. Quite often they are so employed for twenty-four hours on a stretch, with no interruption for rest.

An ordinary laundry, owned by two men and employing no outside help, will earn, as an average, about $1,000 a year, or say $500 for each proprietor. Such an establishment will readily sell for $1,400, the purchase carrying with it all territorial rights.

The washing industry, now so largely followed by Chinamen in this country, is an entirely new vocation to them. They know nothing about it when they come to America, but very quickly master the trade under the tutelage of some "cousin" already in the business. But they have the business thoroughly systematized, and no man is considered competent to earn wages at it until he understands it in all its details. These include marking, checking, booking, making the solutions, washing, boiling, drying, sprinkling, ironing, polishing, bundling and delivering. The average Chinaman will acquire all this in about a month, and is then ready for employment or to set up a laundry on his own account.

CHAPTER VII.

PECULIAR INDUSTRIES.

THE MANY VOCATIONS OF CHINATOWN—THEIR VARIANCE FROM AMERICAN METHODS AND IDEAS—THE GOOD AND THE BAD INEXTRICABLY MIXED—THE USEFUL AND THE SUPERSTITIOUS ALIKE RECOGNIZED AS LEGITIMATE AND PROPER.

THERE are many queer, quaint and curious callings that engage the attention of the Chinese, some of them useful and others quite the reverse. Some of them have their counterpart in American industries, but the different manner in which the Chinese practice them is interesting. Some of the pursuits mentioned below are deserving of more extended notice than the limits of this volume permit. But the mention made will serve to show the dense superstition and ignorance which control these strange people.

MEDICAL PRACTICE AND MEDICINES.

The Chinese have their physicians or doctors, but they are a far different class of professional men from Americans or Europeans who wear the same title. The Chinese "doctor" is a graduate of no medical school or college, for none such exist among the educational establishments of his native land. Nor is he subject to any examination test as a prerequisite to receiving a diploma. Indeed, no diploma is issued or required. Any man, however ignorant, is at liberty to set up as a medical practitioner in China, and by his success or non-success he stands or falls. The most prominent are those whose fathers were doctors before them, and from whom they have inherited prescriptions of supposed merit. But there are old women by the hundreds scattered through the rural districts of America, who are far more capable of ministering to the needs of the sick than the most eminent Chinese "doctor." The pharmacopoeia of these women is peculiarly rich in useful roots and herbs of pronounced medicinal value; whereas, the Chinese "doctor" relies almost wholly on remedies that possess no particle of virtue.

The "doctors" under this system, and so those of Chinatown, are their own apothecaries or pharmacists. A peep into one of their drug stores will suggest a witch's cave. There will be seen collections, not merely of dried herbs, but fragments of nearly everything in the mineral and animal kingdom. Fresh tops of stag horns, dried red spotted lizards, silk worms, moths, tortoise shells, and a hundred other supposedly infallible tonics of like character will be found. If an astringent is needed, here are the bones and teeth of dragons, oyster shells, loadstone, talc, and gold and silver leaf. For purgatives the patient will find verdigris, calcareous spar, satechu, pearls, bear's gall, shavings of rhinoceros horns, turtle shells and a long list of equally efficacious nostrums at his command. Elephant's skin and ivory shavings are provided as antidotes to poison. This queer Chinese pharmacopoeia contains not less than 314 remedies taken from the vegetable kingdom, and 80 from the animal kingdom. All these remedies, good, bad and indifferent, are sanctioned by the medical board at Pekin, and are kept in all well regulated drug stores. Of course the doctor-pharmacist in Chinatown is obliged to import the most of them himself from China.

American philanthropy has recently come to the relief of the dwellers in Chinatown by establishing a free clinic and dispensary, where the sick and afflicted may be treated in a rational and intelligent manner, by practitioners educated to their profession. It may not be appreciated at the outset, but ultimately these victims of superstition and ignorance will discover the superiority of such treatment over the incantations and senseless doses of their own illiterate "doctors."

A STRING BAND.

The usual string band of the Chinese is composed of six pieces. A cracked drum, played with two sticks, is the leading instrument. It is played by the leader of the band and serves as a time marker. A long-handled banjo, with three strings, comes next. Its handle is about three feet in length, and one and one-quarter inches in diameter. The drum of the banjo is covered on either side with the skin of a snake. Its music contains two octaves. The moon banjo is another of the instruments. The drum of this banjo resembles a moon, with a handle the same as an ordinary banjo, but much shorter. It has four strings, but the strings are set in pairs; therefore, it gives the same sound as if played with two strings. Its construction is very simple. If you wish to make one, or one almost like it, buy a common American wooden basin, put a thin piece of wood over the top of the basin, and add the handle to it. It

A CHINESE BAND.

would be a perfect moon banjo of the Chinese style. Next the fiddle. It is the shape of a hammer, has two strings and a bow of horsehair. In use the bow is to be kept between the two strings and constantly greased with rosin. The music of this contrivance covers one and one-half octaves, and is of a very squeaky nature. The alto violin is the shape of a wooden mallet. It is played with two strings and a bow of horsetail, similar to the squeaky fiddle. Its horsehair is also put between the two strings.

It produces a very queer sound, called by the Chinese "make old sow sad." The Chinese music is written only in two keys—C and G. There is no system to conduct a band by note, as in European music. The player has to perfect himself in his part by practice and trust to his memory. For this reason Chinese music has but few titles and no variations. They play the music to-day as they played it hundreds of years ago—the same tunes, the same instruments and the same manner of playing.

The Chinese people are divided into three classes—first, second and low. Officials, students and farmers form the first class. Merchants, fishermen, messengers and the like compose the second class. Actors, musicians and beggars are classified with the lowest of the three. Chinese musicians are not classified as professional men, and their service is not esteemed much above the ordinary laborer. One Chit is the name of the manager of the band in the picture. He plays the drum.

A JEWELRY STORE.

Up a steep flight of stairs at No. 4 Doyers Street is the only Chinese jeweler in Chinatown. As you enter the door your presence is announced to the proprietor by a bell which hangs to the top of the door and rings when anyone enters. It is a little bit of a place, not more than six feet square and is shut off from the rest of the apartment by a partition and wire screen. The space behind the screen against the wall is lined with all the tools of the jeweler. The bench at which the jeweler works runs the entire length of the place, and is littered with old pipe bowls which he has for repair. At one end is a glass cabinet which contains ivory bracelets, pipe bowls, ear-rings, etc. Ching Chang Heo is the proprietor of the place, and he has been established here for about ten years. He is an engraver and carver of ivory and turns out many beautiful things from this highly prized substance. He makes anything in the jewelry line, uses nothing but 24-carat gold, and does a business of about $5,000 a year.

A CHINESE STORE.

At 16 Doyers Street is the store of Soy Kee Company, which will serve as a fair sample of the mercantile establishments of Chinatown. It is a small place, about 8 feet by 15. It is very clean and the shelves on the four sides are neatly packed with everything that the Chinese use, from children's toys to the most costly furs. In this small space there is a stock valued at $10,000, which embraces silks, woolens, furs, hats, coats, jewelry, pipes, crockery, musical instruments, Chinese ornaments, candy, tinware, lanterns, baskets, and in fact everything that is used by the Chinese. The business done amounts to a good many thousand dollars a year.

PAINTING AND LITHOGRAPHING

At No. 1 Doyers Street is the shop of Kai Kee, Chinese artist, engraver, lithographer and sign painter. This is a small store about 6x15 feet in dimensions. The walls are covered with colored pictures cut from the New York papers, and Chinese lithographs. Signs are scattered all about the place, and a lithographing press occupies a good part of the floor space in one corner of the shop.

Kai Kee was born in Hung Shan, China, and is about 35 years of age. He has been in New York about four years. He learned his trade in Hong Kong. He does most of the work required in Chinatown and for the laundrymen. He can paint signs as well as any New

York painter, as is evidenced by those seen in his place. He also makes wood cuts and is a very busy man.

Kai Kee is fairly well educated, both in English and Chinese, and is considered by the Americans, as well as the Chinese, to be a first-class designer and engraver either of figures, landscapes or trade marks. He is interested in American as well as Chinese politics, and in half an hour's talk with him his listener will hear as much about the politics of the Flowery Kingdom as Li Hung Chang himself could tell.

A BAKE SHOP.

In the building, 16 Doyers Street, is Hee Jan, Chinese baker and confectioner, whose place is about 8 feet in width and 15 or 20 feet in depth. Here all kinds of Chinese cakes and pastries are made and sold. Hee Jan employs two helpers, and supplies all the Chinese restaurants and private families in Chinatown. He bakes everything fresh every day, and his annual income is about $5,000 a year. Hee Jan was born in Canton, China, and came here from San Francisco about ten years ago.

"MELLICAN" EATING HOUSE.

At No. 3 Doyers Street is the best American restaurant in Chinatown. It is owned and conducted by Wing Sing, and has been established about 13 years. The place has seating capacity for 28 persons and contains seven tables. There are employed in the restaurant, beside the owner, a cook, two kitchenmen, and three waiters, all Chinese. It is frequented by such Chinese as like "Mellican" cooking, and by the whites of the neighborhood. It is as clean as any of the restaurants in that region of the city, and the business done amounts to about $500 a week. The bill of fare is written both in Chinese and English, and is the same as is found in ordinary restaurants. Everything is served from ham and eggs to turkey.

There are two other such restaurants in basements in Chinatown, one at No. 12 Pell, and the other at No. 22 Pell Street, but their combined business does not equal that of Wing Sing's establishment.

PIG ROASTING.

Pig roasting is a regular trade among the Chinese because of the fondness of those people for that particular meat. Next to rice, pig's meat is probably the most popular dish of their ordinary diet. Naturally, therefore, its preparation for the table becomes a matter of much concern. Young pigs roasted whole are considered the acme of prepared meats. Hence the cook who undertakes its preparation must be an expert in his business. Pigs used for roasting, according to an authority on Chinese cookery, should weigh about sixty pounds. They must be fresh killed and dressed with care. The skin must be thoroughly scraped and cleaned, and the entrails carefully removed. The entire carcass, including the head, tail and feet, with the tongue and ears, is used, each part being supposed to possess a particular relish which it imparts to the whole. A mixture of bean sauce and allspice is added for flavoring. While cooking it is basted with honey mixed with brandy. When done it should be well browned and crisp. About two and a half hours are required for the cooking, and if the above directions are closely followed, the appearance and fragrance of the meat when taken from the oven will be enough to tempt the appetite of the most pronounced gastronomist.

PIG ROASTING OVEN.

The Chinese restaurants have a special oven in which to roast pigs. It is built of brick, round, and slightly conical in form, 3 feet high and about 4½ feet in diameter at the base, which is fitted as a fire box with a door for the admission of fuel. The top is open and provided with a close fitting cover which can be removed for the placing of the meat within, or to watch and attend it while cooking. Only a wood fire is permissible for heating these ovens.

CHINESE PEDLERS.

There are from 25 to 40 Chinamen in this city who make a business of catering to the wants of their countrymen scattered throughout the metropolitan area, or say within a radius of thirty miles, taking Chinatown for a center. There are scattered throughout this region about 13,000 Chinese—laundrymen, laborers and others—all having a fondness for the peculiar viands of their native land. These scattered Chinamen live by themselves in their several localities away from Chinatown, and ordinarily are dependent upon the groceries and meat stores in their neighborhood for the provisions they require. To supply their special wants these caterers, or more properly, pedlers, are called into requisition and find abundant and profitable business. These pedlers carry huge wicker baskets upon their shoulders containing their stock in trade. In these baskets will be found vegetables, squashes, fresh fish, fresh pork, condiments and substantially everything that is found in a Chinese store. The pedlers carry a burden that would make a mule stagger. Their baskets frequently contain 200 and 300 pounds weight of merchandise, with which they travel miles with apparent ease. They replenish their stock every night, and start out on their tours as early as 5.30 A. M. Each one has his well defined territory to cover, and permits no intrusion. The prices he charges for his wares will average 10 per cent. less than the merchant in Chinatown can afford to sell at. For this reason the regular merchant is his bitter enemy and denounces him as a "stinging bee." The pedlers, of course, have their own union, which arranges and assigns the districts for each and the prices to be charged. The individual pedler usually lives in his own district, and buys his goods at first hand. He is not known to nor licensed by the Mayor's marshal.

AN ACTOR AND HIS FAMILY.

Leung Bow, the famous female impersonator, when in San Francisco, attracted at least fifty of the prettiest belles of Chinatown in that city with his size. But out of the whole lot he liked Lin He the best. Lin He herself was a slave at the time, but she had more sense than the average slave possesses. She had saved up $800 and put it away as her own money. She pleaded hard with Bow to redeem her body from her master. The price set upon her was $1,200, and she wanted Bow to put up $400 and she would make up the balance. It did not take Bow long to decide the question. As soon as the money was paid the pair walked off, arm in arm, going direct to the playhouse on Clay Street. Mrs. Bow found life lonesome, so she resolved to buy a girl for her comfort. The girl was bought, Mrs. Bow paying the price for her. Mrs. Bow now considers her family comfortable. They came to New York in 1895. Mr. Bow is engaged in a playhouse at No. 5 Doyers Street. They reside in the second basement of the same building, Mrs. Bow assisting her husband in hitting the pipe. The little girl, Annie, helps her father make cigarettes.

FORTUNE TELLING.

"Professor" Leung Ding Shin is a fortune teller, a distinct and recognized calling among the people of his race, and one that is well patronized by all classes and for all purposes. Leung is one of the foremost young men of Chinatown. His office fronts on Mott Street, above the entrance to which flies a flag of Leung's own designing, on which is displayed in Chinese characters this legend:

Professor Leung,
Kwa Ming Yu Shan.

The interpretation thereof would read: "Professor Leung, Fortune Telling as God's Divine." The heathen, although they do believe in a supreme being, do not consider it sinful to take God's name in vain. Many of them, in their ignorance and superstition, actually believe that a fortune teller has divine wisdom to foretell events.

Professor Leung displays in his room his card of prices for various professional services. The list of services is

LEUNG DING SHIN.

about a yard in length. Following are some specimens from it:

Foretelling fortunes	$1.00
Foretelling love	2.50
Foretelling co-partnership	1.50
Foretelling marriage	2.50
Lost and found	1.50
Information to capture runaway lover	3.00
History of one's future life	10.00

And so on through all the phases of human anxiety and doubt. It is a great business, and Leung gives to it, apparently, strict attention.

Lo Ping and Jo Sung.

A CHINESE MONEY LENDER.

Lo Ping, "the loan man," is a merchant of high standing in Chinatown, a member of the Lee Wah Lung Company, at 10 Pell Street. He is a lucky fellow—what his countrymen call Man Ngnang Kai Chuck Tin Chong—"a blind chicken bang against a worm." Three years ago he was but an ordinary laundryman; now he is coining money at the northerly end of Pell Street. If he has no pullback he is destined to become a wealthy man, and one of the most prominent in Chinatown. He does a banking business for his "cousins." As a rule Chinamen do not put much faith in "Mellican" banks, prefering to trust their own people. So many of them entrust their money to Lo Ping, who invests it in loans to whoever wants to borrow and has good security to offer. His borrowers are largely men who want to buy laundries. His rate of interest is 5 per cent. a month to those who want money for the purchase of a wife. He generally has money in hand for all comers; all that is necessary to effect the loan being to go before the Mayor of Chinatown and draw up and sign a borrowing contract. Such contracts are sacred among the Chinese. At the end of every month he will get his 5 per cent. interest, or if not, all he has to do is to notify the mayor, who will then summon the Chong Wah Gong Shaw, bring the parties before it and give a decision of the case in his presence.

A LOTTERY AGENT.

Jo Sung, "The Plug," as the Chinese call him, whose picture accompanies that of Lo Ping, is a prosperous lottery agent at 18 Mott Street. His business is said to amount to $200 a day, the commission on which at 7 per cent. brings him in a revenue of $14 a day. He is a very liberal fellow, giving just as freely as he receives. He occasionally takes a trip to China, but does not stay away long. The Pell Street women hang about him in bunches. They call him "Plum Pudding."

The conjunction of these two personages in one photograph very strikingly illustrates the peculiar moral and business ideas that prevail in Chinatown. The prosperous banker is hand in hand with the thrifty lottery agent, and each is alike respected in that strange community.

TWO CHINESE ACROBATS.

Dai Sa Kwong and Dai Sa Loong are the most famous Chinese acrobats who have ever regaled the denizens of

Chinatown, where for two seasons previous to their departure for San Francisco, they reigned supreme favorites in the Chinese Opera House, at 5 and 7 Doyers Street.

The Chinaman is not much given to levity, yet the fantastic antics of these two acrobats, who are father and son, have made all Chinatown expand in a broad grin while witnessing their great feats of strength interwoven with a by-play of native comedy, which has made them the envied of their fellow professionals.

During the summer season of 1897 they made their appearance at the larger of the seaside concert halls at Coney Island, where thousands witnessed their performance. It was here that a romance, which for a time threatened to separate the doting father and his son permanently, first developed. Dai Sa Loong, who is but 28 years of age, and possesses well developed ideas on the Americanization of the Chinese, blossomed into a dude of the first watering place order. And it was here, too, that he fell the victim for the first time to the wiles of the "Mellican Gal." Loong's raiment was of the finest, his neckties of the nattiest and he evinced a fondness for diamond jewelry. All of which made its impression on the heart and mind of one Miss Laura Jones, herself a seaside thespian. Her fancy for Loong soon developed into a passion more tender and deep, and it was not long before the cooing of the couple furnished food for seaside gossips. The love-making was all unknown to father Kwong, who, when he learned that his son and heir had taken unto himself another partner, became furious. Rumor reached the old man that Loong and Laura had been wed and were living together at one of the summer hotels. He made dire threats of disowning his son and disinheriting him of his portion of a $10,000 fortune. For a time the young man wavered twixt love and duty. He weighed his affection for his inamorata against the $10,000 in glistening gold, and finally for-

KWONG AND LOONG.

sook his love to rejoin the solicitous parent and accompany him on a tour to California, where they are now gathering new laurels in "The Home of the First Born."

CHAPTER VIII.

TONSORIAL ARTISTS.

A NECESSARY CALLING AMONG THE CHINESE—UNIVERSALITY OF HEAD SHAVING—HOW THE BARBERS WORK—THE PECULIAR TOOLS THEY USE—PRICES CHARGED.

HE universal custom with Chinamen of shaving the head and wearing a queue makes the barber's trade a large and flourishing one. At the present day every Chinaman, who is loyal to the government at Pekin and who has not discarded the superstitions and traditions which rule that country, shaves his head, with the exception of the crown, where the hair is allowed to grow its full length. This hair is carefully and neatly braided and allowed to fall down the back, forming what many irreverent outsiders call the "pig-tail." Great pride is taken in having as long and thick a queue as possible, and when nature has been sparing in her natural growth, the deficiency is supplemented by the insertion of silk in the plait. One very rarely sees a queue that is all hair. In the majority of cases more than half of its length is

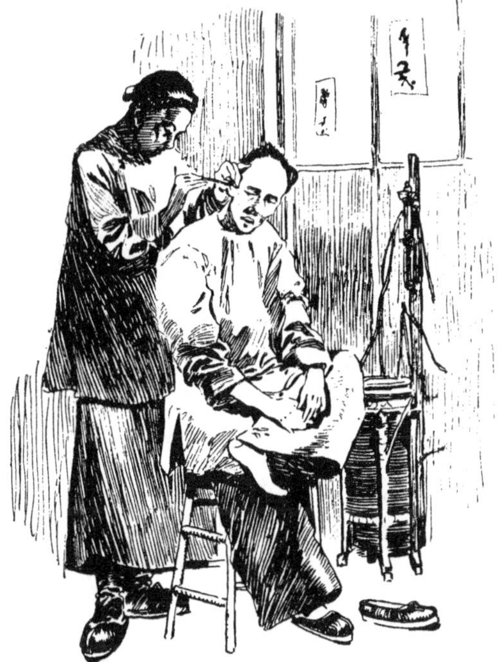

CHINESE BARBER AT WORK.

merely braided silk, or not infrequently some cheaper material. Among all classes great value is attached to this appendage, which is considered a mark of good standing, and no greater opprobrium can be cast upon a man than to designate him as Mo-pien—"tailless."

As a general rule the head is shaved about once in every ten days, though those who are particular as to their appearance shave oftener, while the shiftless ones, the poorer classes and criminals, frequently shave but once a month.

Besides the barber shops, itinerant barbers find plenty of patronage in the land of queues. These latter carry all the implements of their trade, together with a stool for the customer to sit upon, suspended at the end of a bamboo pole slung on the shoulders. They are ready for business wherever they may chance to meet a customer, merely withdrawing to the side of the street to avoid the pressure and jostling of the passing crowd. Not many of these street barbers are met in our Chinatown, but they are quite numerous in San Francisco, while in China they are as common as are the regular barber shops.

In the New York Chinatown the barbers occupy small rooms for shops, situated usually in the basement or upper floors of buildings. Economic considerations forbid their use of the ground floor. There is one of these shops, typical of all of them, which occupies a room scarcely ten feet square, in which, when the writer visited it, he found three barbers at work upon as many customers seated on stools, while three others stood waiting their turn. Across about half the room, and suspended but barely three feet from the ceiling, was a platform, or sort of gallery, on which the barbers slept at night. The height of the room afforded merely scant standing room under this gallery. And this is considered a "first-class" shop. A single average American working alone in such a contracted space would apprehend stifling; yet here were nine men—three of them working there all day and sleeping there at night, and six of them required to remain from one to two hours, and yet none of them manifested the slightest inconvenience because of the restricted space and fetid atmosphere.

Hot water, with no soap, is used by these Oriental barbers in their shaving, the operation including not merely the removal of the stubble on the scalp, but the down, or more sturdy growth of beard, on the cheeks and chin, as well as all intruding hair on the neck. But a Chinaman's beard is not a formidable crop. His face is usually singularly devoid of hairy growth, while whiskers are rarely seen. A mustache, if it can be grown, is only permissable for a man who has arrived at the age of forty years. On the occasion of the death of a near relative the hair is allowed to remain unshaven for a period of one hundred days as a sign of mourning, and for the whole mourning period—twenty-seven months—in the case of the death of a parent.

A sketch of the implements used by the barber is given herewith. The razor has a short blade, shaped something like a rounded isosceles triangle, the long side being the cutting edge. The cleansing of the ears forms an important part of the operation of shaving, and calls for the use of other tools, as shown in the cut. The inside of the ear is not merely shaved, but it is thoroughly scraped and the orifice cleansed as well, the operation finishing with a sweep of a duck's down brush. The sensation produced by the skillful application of this brush in the ear is described as quite electrical. The whole shaving process and dressing of the queue requires from an hour to an hour and a half. The Chinatown barber's fee for his service is usually fifty cents, though some of them work for less. The merchant and laundrymen are the most frequent customers. Those employed in questionable or dishonest pursuits shave less frequently, considering it unlucky to have a cleanly shaven head. When a professional gambler has his head freshly shaven he will not go near the gaming table, remaining away until the stubble is again manifest.

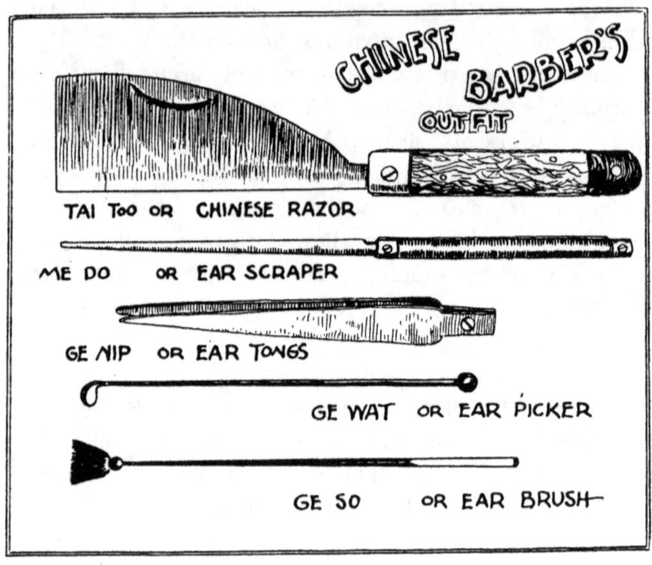

CHAPTER IX.

TILLERS OF THE SOIL.

THE "FARMERS" WHO PROVIDE CHINATOWN WITH ITS PECULIAR VEGETABLES—WHERE THEY WORK AND HOW THEY LIVE—AN INDUSTRIOUS BODY OF MONGOLIANS.

EVERY tiller of the soil in China is a farmer, whether he cultivates a large farm or merely grows garden truck on half an acre of ground. The distinction between a farmer and a gardener seems to be unknown to them. And so it happens that the Chinamen in the suburbs of New York who make their living by raising the peculiar vegetables most affected by the Chinese palate, as well as the more common kinds in general use, are called farmers. They are an honest, industrious and hard-working class, and deserving of all the recompense they may get for their toil. They work from the earliest dawn of daylight until it becomes too dark in the evening to see to work longer.

There are seven "farms," or gardens, under cultivation by these people on Long Island, each from five to six acres in extent. The ground so used is leased from the white owners. The farms are conducted under firm or company names, as are the mercantile establishments in Chinatown, each being composed of three or four partners and employing six or seven hands besides. But partners and hands live and work together, and would be indistinguishable in American eyes. Of the "farms," five are located in the vicinity of Astoria, and one each at Steinway and Flatbush. They are known as Hen Shang Yen, Sam Yek Yen, Hai Lee Yen, Mon Lee Yen, Yow Lee Yen, all at Astoria; Tai Ping Yen at Flatbush, and Wong Lee Yen at Steinway. The proprietors and their employees live together in cabins on their respective farms.

These farmers dress no differently from the ordinary Chinese laborer, except that they wear fearful and wonderful hats, such as a sentimental fancy might term picturesque. They are made of bamboo, with rims about three feet in diameter, and are shaped like shallow tin pans. They serve the double purpose of sunshades and umbrellas.

These Oriental tillers of the soil disdain American tools, preferring implements to which they and their ancestors have been accustomed for thousands of years. Their principal implement is a long bamboo-handled hoe, which answers the purpose of a plow, a spade, a rake and a hoe proper. With it they dig up the ground at the outset; then pulverize it and mix whatever fertilizers they may use; shape and prepare the beds; plant the seeds, and, when the crop is growing, cultivate it.

These hardy toilers, like all other followers of a common pursuit among the Chinese, have their own union. The union does not have a great deal to say or do, but it controls the particular industry of its members. It regulates the wages to be paid to employees, the manner of packing and marketing their product, the prices at which it may be sold, and so on. Their regulations are few and simple but none the less binding on all concerned. Whatever the union says is the law for all their class. If consumers do not fancy the prices it puts upon the fruit of the soil as raised by its members, so much the worse for the consumer; he gets no fresh vegetables. The truck raised by these farmers is mainly taken by the Chinese pedlers of this city and Brooklyn, who in turn dispose of it to the merchants and restaurants of Chinatown, and to the laundrymen in all quarters of the city.

The Chinese farmer requires as much industry on the part of the soil he cultivates as he puts out himself. He allows it no idleness or rest, at least during the growing season, and that he stretches to its utmost possible limit. No sooner is one crop gathered than another is planted in its place. In this way three or more crops are produced from the same plot of ground during a season, each crop being forced forward by all the arts of the trade—careful removal of weeds, frequent watering, skillful cultivating, and whatever may minister to rapid growth and development.

The first crop produced is a tender little plant which looks very much like clover, called Yun Tsoi. It is highly esteemed by the Chinamen as a soup ingredient. It only requires about twenty days to produce it ready for market. It is, of course, pulled when yet green. When about five inches above ground it is considered in condition for use. It is then gathered, tied in bundles weighing about one pound each, and is ready for market. The price for it is twelve cents a bundle at wholesale, and it retails at fifteen cents a bundle. Yun Tsoi usually makes its appearance in the market about the first of April.

The second crop from these farms is usually ready about the 15th of April. It is, in plain English, kale, but the Chinese produce two varieties of it—Kai Tsoi and Bok Tsoi. The former is green kale and the latter white. Both are alike boiled in soup. They require about thirty days' time from planting to attain perfection. The plant is larger and more bushy than Yun Tsoi, and is sold cheaper, not being considered such a luxury. One and a half pounds are put in a bunch. It sells at six cents a bunch wholesale and eight cents retail.

German sugar peas are produced about the 20th of April. This is not a vegetable, as might be supposed, but an ingredient used in making Chop Suey.

In the latter part of June vegetables proper begin to come in from these farms. The first to make its appearance is called Sze Kwa (or sponge squash). About the same time Fu Kwa (or balsam apple) and Chit Kwa (hairy squash) come also. These several varieties of squash are used only for soup purposes, the Fu Kwa being especially esteemed. It has a bitter taste and is supposed to contain quinine in its composition. It is sometimes used as a condiment in stewing chicken, making pork soup and frying lobsters. The Oriental epicure counts it of great value in toning up the system. The

SOME OF THE PRODUCTS.

Sze Kwa is only fit to eat when young and tender. Its average weight is about a pound and a half. When ripe its form is like the peculiar sponge the Chinese use when bathing—hence its name. Chit Kwa is picked when it will weigh a pound and a half; when fully ripe it weighs from twenty-five to forty pounds. It is used either in soup or is made into a sweetmeat like citron.

Of course there are other vegetables grown by the Chinese. Indeed, they produce nearly everything that is indigenous to the soil, especially such as find favor with Chinese gastronomists. Especial mention is made only of those unfamiliar to Americans.

CHAPTER X.

CHINATOWN'S OPERA HOUSE.

THE ONLY PLEASURE RESORT OF CHINATOWN—SINGULARITIES OF THE CHINESE DRAMA—THE COMPANY NOW OCCUPYING THE BOARDS THERE..

HE principal place of amusement in Chinatown is the theater, or, more correctly, "Chinese Opera House." This is located at 5 Doyers Streèt. It is not a very pretentious playhouse, but is quite characteristic. The main building is occupied as an American lodging house, the theater finding its accommodation in the basement. This is fitted up with a stage or platform across the rear end, and, like all Chinese theaters, is innocent of curtains or scenery. The wall back of it is elaborately painted in high, bright colors, representing birds, beasts and reptiles. In the center is a painted joss. On either side of the joss are doors, through one of which the actors enter, and through the other take their exit when they have finished their respective parts. The orchestra is seated on the back part of the stage, immediately in front of the pictured joss. The auditorium is filled with rough wooden benches, enough to accommodate possibly 500 people. At the right of the stage is an enclosure, or private box, which is usually occupied by white people and slumming parties. Two other boxes are located in the corners of the extreme front of the house.

A peculiar feature of this, and all other Chinese theaters, is the sliding scale of prices charged for admission. The regular prices are twenty-five and fifty cents, and one dollar for a seat in the private box. Should a belated Chinaman wish to enter an hour after the performance has begun, the doorkeeper will cut the rate for him about one-half. Half an hour later he will again dissect the figure for the benefit of the tardy visitor, who may then gain admission for ten or fifteen cents.

The Chinese drama has been so often described that it seems unnecessary to say anything further regarding it in this connection. The plays generally represent some historical train of events, extending through the reign of a dynasty, or an interesting national epoch. Very little is left to the imagination of the spectator, and the literal text of the drama does not develop a plot with anything like the rapidity and dispatch which characterize our American or English plays. The Chinese play is emphatically a physical delineation of events from beginning to end. The most trivial occurrences of life are faithfully portrayed, and at times very questionable and obscene practices are represented, but not often. Two or three months are generally consumed before all the acts of a play are finished.

When one of the characters in the play falls upon the stage, either from the effect of a blow or a fainting attack, supernumeraries at once step forward and place under his head a small block of wood or other substance for a pillow. A slain person lies in this way until the end of the scene, when he coolly walks off the stage in full view of the entire audience. The orchestra keeps up an infernal and ear-splitting din with gongs, tom-toms, Chinese guitars, fiddles, triangles and cymbals throughout the entire dialogue. Not infrequently the performers, when not actually engaged in the scene, sit and lounge about the stage, smoking, munching sugar cane or sweetmeats, and at times even crossing the stage while a scene is in progress.

The audience at a Chinese theater never applauds. Occasionally a half-suppressed murmur of satisfaction is heard, but no clapping of hands, stamping of feet, whistles or cat-calls are indulged in. The men sit with their hats on, generally perching on the backs of the benches, or wander about the house talking with friends and acquaintances in an ordinary tone of voice. Smoking and eating are constantly in progress in all parts of the house, and the practice of running in and out is freely indulged.

The costumes of the actors are grotesque, often hideous in the extreme. Occasionally a little dancing diversifies the play, but this is an exercise never indulged in by the Chinese off the stage. They cannot understand why people should exhaust themselves in this way when they can employ actors to do it for them. Moreover, as in Chinese society there is no intercourse between men and women, no opportunity is presented for dancing, unless it be among "stags," and that sort of thespian indulgence is not highly appreciated by any people. But while not much dancing is shown on the Chinese stage, yet they do sometimes exhibit rare feats in tumbling, turning cart wheels, feats of juggling, and so on.

Chinese actors are not held in high esteem by their compatriots, the calling being considered rather the reverse of respectable, whatever its emoluments may be, and these are not always niggardly. Women are but rarely seen upon the stage, the female characters being assumed commonly by men. The "starring" system is unknown among them.

The Doyers Street Theater is conducted by the Chay Ding Quay Company, of which Chin You is the manager. It was a highly prosperous enterprise so long as Sunday performances were given. But since the Parkhurst period the city police have been more active, and the theater is closed on that day. As Sunday brings unusual throngs to Chinatown, the most of whom are pleasure seekers and would gladly patronize the theater, its enforced closure on that day is a serious loss to the proprietors.

The company now performing here is composed exclusively of talent imported direct from China for this house. The company, including actors, attendants, musicians, etc., numbers about two score people. The principal actor, or leading man, is Lee Sang. He receives a stipend of $1,500 a year, payable in American gold, which is considered an exceptionally large salary. In addition, his board and lodging are furnished him. From this the salary list runs down rapidly to the lowest, which is $300 a year and "found," also.

CHAPTER XI.

CHINESE GAMBLING.

PASSION OF THE CELESTIALS FOR GAMES OF CHANCE—DESCRIPTIONS OF SOME OF THEIR GAMES—FAN TAN—LOTTERIES—THE RIDDLE GAME—THEY ARE ALL "OFFICIALLY" RECOGNIZED.

HE Chinese are naturally and constitutionally the most invcterate of gamblers. Almost all of them gamble, and their code of morality places no embargo on the practice. They only wonder that the laws of this country should forbid what they consider so harmless and proper an amusement. They do not indulge in their games of chance solely for money-getting purposes, though that may furnish the inspiration in many cases, but rather for excitement and pleasure. And the gaming being perfectly lawful and proper under the laws of their native land, and they having indulged in it from childhood, they cannot readily appreciate that it is an unlawful practice in this country. Of course the older immigrants and those professional gamblers who own and control the games know that it is a forbidden practice, and for that reason surround it with so much secrecy, and submit to the blackmail levied upon them by the highbinders for "protection" in its indulgence; and sometimes blind the eyes of an intrusive policeman with liberal payments for not disturbing them. They can compel them to pay generously for this "protection" because of the universal disposition of their countrymen to patronize the games, which makes the business highly lucrative.

Fan tan is the game most popular and most generally patronized by these people. An idea of the extent to which it is played may be gathered from the fact that an enumeration recently made showed no less than eighty places in Chinatown where the game is regularly in operation. Each and all of these places pay the Hip Sing Tong, or Highbinders' Society, tribute in money for the privilege of carrying on the game without molestation or disturbance. This tribute, or "protection money," is levied according to a fixed scale. Games located in basements or on the ground or main floor, are assessed $15 a week per table. Sixty of these tables are in existence, besides ten policy shops. This money is collected with regularity every week by a regular collector whose name, as well as his occupation and personality, are well known. It is a common belief that some of the money reaches the hands of the police, though on that point there is no direct evidence beyond the inference to be gathered from the fact that the patrolmen do not discover the games which are so well known to everybody else. A story is told that one of the proprietors, whose place is at 28 Pell Street, distrusting the collector, insisted that a former Mayor of Chinatown, and now representing the Hip Sing Tong, should come and receive the money, whereupon the patrolman on the beat, an officer of the Elizabeth Street Station, called on the proprietor of the game and told him he had better pay the regular collector. This the proprietor persistently refused to do, declaring he would only pay the police direct or the ex-mayor. The truthfulness of this story is not vouched for, nor is the outcome of the alleged controversy known.

When a fan tan game is to be started ten men usually club together, each contributing $30. Out of this money the "joint," or place where the game is to be conducted, is secured and fitted up. The rent will be about $15 a week, which is invariably required in advance. Then the table is purchased at a cost of $5. This is about all the furniture required. Gas is needed; for the supplying of which the gas company requires a deposit of $10. "Protection" money must also be paid in advance, and that is at least $15. The remaining money, about $240 or $250, is reserved for the bank, or capital of the game. The "joint" is then ready for business.

The various fan tan games of Chinatown are all subject to the control of the Fan Tan Hong, or syndicate, as it would be called in English. This is a voluntary organization of Chinamen of prominence and influence who undertake the regulation of the game in general; adjust disputes between warring "joints;" fix the number of games to be allowed, and exercise general supervision over that particular form of gambling. The open character of the game, and its entire reputability and lawfulness, in Chinese estimation, is manifested by the standing of this Fan Tan Hong or syndicate. It has its headquarters in the building of the Chong Wah Gong Shaw, or Chinatown's City Hall, and conducts its business as openly and with as much show of right and authority as does the Chong Wah Gong Shaw itself, or any of the several trade organizations.

Every fan tan game employs one lookout man, one dealer and one banker. The duties of these several officials are obvious from their titles. The paraphernalia of the game consists of the "Board," a plain, square piece of zinc or tin, ten or twelve inches square, the sides being numbered I, II, III, IV. This is laid on one end of a common table about which the players gather, the dealer sitting in front of the board. A short stick, about the size of a chop stick, but twice the length, with which the dealer manipulates the "cash," or pieces with which the game is played; a number of "cash"—small circular brass pieces with a square hole in the center (one or two hundred of these are used)—and a "cover"—a round brass vessel sufficiently large to cover the "cash" used—constitute the outfit.

On the opposite page is given a cut illustrating the manner of playing the game, and the paraphernalia employed.

FAN-TAN PLAYERS AND UTENSILS.

The game being ready, the dealer takes a handful of the "cash" from the box in which they are kept and carelessly lays them in front of him, placing the cover over them, so that they may not be counted or estimated. The bets are then made, each bettor placing upon the board the amount of money he purposes to bet. The dealer then proceeds to separate from the common pile with his stick four pieces of "cash" at a time, the game turning on the last draw, whether it be an odd or even number of pieces. This, however, has its modifications, as whether it will be one, two, three or four pieces. And, again, betting may be made on one number as against the other three, or two numbers against two, and so on. Whatever number of pieces remain for the last draw, that number wins.

In playing, the money bet is placed upon the board. The location in which it is placed determines the bet. If a player places one dollar on the corner of the board formed by the intersection of the two sides III and IV, he is betting against numbers I and II. If he loses, his loss is one dollar. If he wins he receives ninety-three cents, the remaining seven cents being "Soi" or water. Seven per cent. of all winnings are retained by the bank to defray the expenses and for profit, and is known as Soi.

If the player places one dollar squarely on the side marked I, he plays that number against the other three. If he loses, he only loses his one dollar; but if he wins, which he does if only one piece remains for the last draw, he wins $3.00 less seven per cent., or $2.79 net.

When one dollar is placed on a number, "Chang How," then the bet is only against the opposite number, as I against III or II against IV. The number on which the money is placed is the winning number for the bettor, and the opposite number is his loser. It is an even bet, but he can only win should his chosen number come out, or lose should the opposite number appear. If neither number comes, then the bet is off and the player may withdraw his stakes.

The banker takes in all the money that is lost to the house and pays the winning of the bettors.

The lookout watches the board for any carelessness or mistakes in placing bets; that no bettor takes up money not belonging to him, and that the transactions are all correct.

The usual limit of the game is five cents as a minimum bet and $500 for the highest. The average bet is $1, though hundreds of more impecunious ones bet half a dollar, a quarter or even a nickel, if that is all they can command. As many may play as can find place around the table, and the room is quite frequently crowded with eager onlookers, who, perhaps, have no money with which to play.

When the fear of the police was not so great as it is now it was the custom to have a man stationed at the street door to call out to the crowds in the street and to passers, Moi Han La! which meant "The game is now open; come in and play!" Now, on the contrary, a watchman is placed at the door to keep out white people, unless vouched for, and also to give notice of the approach of the police. But this is a mere pretence, as the police very rarely trouble the games, though their location and notoriety are known through Chinatown.

CHINESE LOTTERY.

Lottery is another form of gambling affected by the Chinese, though not by any means to the extent of fan tan. The Chinese lottery is very different from the lottery of the white people. It has no great capital; offers no grand prize, nor in fact any prizes at all. It is more like the policy so well known among the negroes and the lower classes of white people in this country. It is conducted by three persons—the conductor, or manager, a secretary and an assistant secretary. The conductor manages the drawings; the secretary receives the money and records the bets; the assistant secretary has charge of the drawing board, and marks out with brush and red ink the winning numbers. This "drawing board" is merely a placard bearing 80 Chinese characters, arranged in columns of four characters each, duplicates of which on small sheets are furnished to the players as tickets.

A LOTTERY TICKET.

When the drawing is ready the manager tears each of the characters off the board, rolling them up separately in snug, tight wads, which are then placed in a tin can and thoroughly shaken and mixed. He then draws them out one at a time without opening them, and divides them equally among four pots or receptacles.

Then a lot is drawn to determine which pot shall be opened. If pot or lot three is thus selected, the pot or lot so chosen becomes the one from which the drawing is to be made. The manager then proceeds to draw out the wadded characters from the pot so indicated. These he opens as drawn, calling out as he does so the names of the inscribed character or letter. This is then stuck on the drawing board in the place from which it was originally torn. The assistant marks out the winning numbers with red ink.

The methods of playing lottery are various, but the simplest is that the player selects any ten numbers from the eighty, either all in one column, in a row or otherwise, as he pleases. If five of the selected letters come out among the twenty drawn by the manager, the one who selected the ten wins double the money he may have wagered. If he has selected six of the drawn letters he wins $20 for one; if seven, $200 for one; if eight, $1,000 for one; if nine, $2,000 for one; if ten or all the drawn letters, the winning would be $4,000 for each dollar invested. But no such luck has ever been experienced by any player. Indeed, rarely does a player hit even five of the letters. If any number less than five have been selected the player wins nothing, but loses his investment, which may have been five cents or five dollars.

The Chinese lottery players are ten times more superstitious than the American players. They rely unhesitatingly upon their dreams. For instance, if one dreams about a dead man he will select a letter for the lottery drawing which will indicate death. If he dreams about girls in bed he will select a whole row of letters containing the one letter bearing the character "girls." There are many Chinamen who have lived in Chinatown for years and have never done any work, but who place their faith wholly on dreams and Joss.

The lotteries of Chinatown, like everything else, have a union. They are all under one common supervision, charge one uniform price for their tickets, pay the same commissions to agents. Each has a capital of $3,000. There are nine of these concerns as follows:

Wing Chung Tai, 10 Mott Street.
Chong Chin Wing, 11 Mott Street.
Hang Chung Tai, 18 Mott Street.
Lin Tai, 17 Mott Street.
Sam Toy, 30 Mott Street.
Yuen Lee, 18 Mott Street.
Foo Kwai Chin, 32 Mott Street.
Wing Yuen Tai, 14 Mott Street.
Lee Ching Chung, 16 Mott Street.

Each lottery has two drawings a day, one at 3.30 P. M. and the other at 9.30 at night. They give employment to about 150 agents, who go around selling the tickets and collecting the bettings, which they turn in to the company employing them. For their part of the work they receive 10 per cent. of the money they collect. But no agent is allowed to collect a commission unless he belongs to the Lottery Agents' Union, the fee for admission to which is $5, or $25 for a life membership. This union extends help to its members when in distress, or when they get into trouble with the police or the lottery managers.

These lotteries, however fairly conducted, are a gigantic swindle, the chances of winning at them being less than in any other game of chance. By careful calculation the game gives the managers 65 per cent of the chances, while the player has but 35 per cent. Some of the poor infatuated players are laundrymen who work hard six days in a week and then squander their earnings on these lopsided lotteries. The man is not known who ever made a respectable winning at any of them, while their victims are numbered by the thousands.

THE RIDDLE GAME, OR TSZ FA.

Anotner form of gambling among the Chinese is that known as the riddle game, riddle policy, or transformation of characters. In this game there are thirty-six chances. Usually the outline figure of a person is drawn and the different parts of the body are marked, every mark representing a chance of the game. A few hours prior to the drawing the dealer gives out a verse something like this:

"The bright light shines over the shadow valley."

Then the persons wishing to play gather and guess as to the meaning of the verse. The letters in the chance always bear the meaning. They stand either for bird, fish, spider, wild cat, tiger, money, strong man, dead body, pretty woman, old maid, etc.

The dealer pastes the letter on a piece of cloth, rolls it up and hangs it on the wall, which means that "the game is hung up." A player may guess any one of the thirty-six chances, and having bet from one to fifty cents, his winning is thirty for one.

He might, for instance, construe the meaning of "shining light" to be a "pretty woman," and if the letter shows this to be a correct guess he wins. The percentage to the house, or dealer, is twenty per cent. The agents for this game have a union known as the Tsz Fa Chong, or Union, which translated means Riddle Game Union. On all money that the agents play for their principals they are allowed 10 per cent., and if they win they get 10 per cent. more from the person for whom they play. Nobody is allowed this commission except those who belong to the Tsz Fa Chong.

There are six games of riddle going on in Chinatown and each has two drawings a day, one at 3.30 o'clock in the afternoon and the other at 9.30 o'clock in the evening, the same as the lotteries. There are twenty-five members of the Tsz Fa Chong. These riddle games do an aggregate business of about $700 a day.

The game is played by the Chinese and the white strumpets of the district as well. It is no uncommon thing to hear one of the white women say she dreamed of a spider, or a pretty woman, etc., the night before, and was going to play riddle on the dream.

There are still other games of chance played in Chinatown, but the foregoing are the ones most largely patronized. Their patronage shows how general is the gaming habit among these people.

CHAPTER XII.

PROSTITUTION.

TRAFFIC IN CHINESE WOMEN—THE DENS OF INFAMY OF CHINATOWN—THE DEPTH OF DEGRADATION—CHIEFLY LOW WHITE WOMEN—THE LOW GUI GOW.

EMALE virtue is a rarity among the Chinese except among the higher classes. The female offspring of the middle and lower classes is considered an inferior being, upon whom parental affection is wasted. She is valued only at the price she will bring either as a wife or mistress. Her chastity is not considered for a moment. Thus Chinamen have quite naturally come to consider prostitution a quite proper sphere for their surplus women.

Only a small-footed woman, one whose feet have been kept from their natural growth by tight bandaging from early childhood, is esteemed virtuous. Such are carefully reared in the concealment of home until disposed of by their parents to become the wives of the sons of respectable families. All big, or natural-footed women, are looked upon with suspicion. Not all of these are common prostitutes, but the demand for women for vile purposes is supplied from this source. These women are sold as early in life as customers can be found for them, either to become wives, mistresses or worse. The only value their parents place upon them is their worth as chattels for any purpose. Hundreds of these women have been brought to America and are held in dens of infamy by those who have purchased them. The highbinders find the traffic in this class of chattels a lucrative occupation.

Happily but few Chinese women have as yet been brought to New York, the prostitutes of our Chinatown being chiefly degraded white women, attracted thither originally by a passion for opium smoking. These miserable creatures the highbinders levy tribute upon, in default of a license to buy and sell them outright, as they do the Chinese women. But the actual slave trade—the importation and sale of Chinese girls right here in the heart of this great city—has already obtained a foothold, and will doubtless grow apace unless resolutely put down by the philanthropy of which we boast so largely. The highbinders are eager for the development of the traffic, and have made some promising beginnings in it. In the spring of 1889, a highbinder bought a girl at Victoria, B. C., for the sum of $1,800. After she was paid for he named her Yen Moy. He brought her to New York with the understanding that she was to become a "Lo Ki," meaning a woman of shame, for the term of two

BIG AND SMALL FOOTED WOMEN.

years and six months, after which time she should be free from her owner. But when the two years and six months had expired, and three months grace had also passed, she was still a slave, because she could still be made profitable to her master. Being free, her earnings became her own; but her master compelled her to give him money to play fan tan and whatever more he needed to pose as a member of Chinatown's Four Hundred. One day his slave awoke to her position and related her tale of woe to Messrs. Huie Kin, Wong Chin Fee, Sue Chung Chew and Joseph M. Singleton, who reported the case to the Gerry Society. This was in the fall of 1891. Miss Yen Moy was rescued from her worse than prison, a room on the top floor of 11 Mott Street. She was finally placed in the hands of Miss Campbell, a Presbyterian missionary, who resided at No. 282 Fulton Street, Brooklyn, where she lived and learned to say the Lord's Prayer, and was afterwards married to Jung Sing, a laundryman.

Female slaves, lot No. 2, were also imported from Victoria, B. C., by a young highbinder named Chu Ngai. The lot consisted of two attractive looking girls named Lin Fung and Song Fung. Lin means "Lilly;" Fung means "Peacock." When the two words are put together, Lin Fung, they mean "As pretty as a peacock and as sweet as a pond lilly." Song Fung means "Twice as pretty as a peacock." The price paid for these girls was $2,000 each. The term of contract was two years. The price might have been less than advertised. As a matter of fact business of this kind is made more profitable by putting the cost of a new girl up to an immense figure to make sure of catching the attention of wealthy customers. That everything might go well with the enterprising dealer they all boarded the Canadian Pacific

A SLAVE GIRL.

train for New York. When they reached Malone, N. Y., they passed the Custom House without the slightest trouble. Finally they reached this city and the girls were placed at 17 Mott Street, where Miss Lin Fung made her permanent residence. She quickly became the reigning beauty of Chinatown. Chinamen are not slow to note female attractions when they see them. Miss Lin Fung made money fast and handed it over to Chu Ngai just as quickly.

But Miss Song Fung soon found life a burden, for Chu Ngai expected to get as much money from her as he did from Lin Fung. She realized she was in a slave prison. She cried hard to Joss for deliverance, but Joss did not hear her prayer. Her eyes began to lose their lustre from weeping. Chu Ngai could see that his "goods" began to show impairment. He planned to sell her before she got worse. South Clark Street, Chicago, was the place Chu Ngai picked out as a market for her. So he went to Chicago to negotiate the sale and get his bargain money. When he returned to New York he found Miss Song Fung still weeping for her woes. Chu Ngai told her that he was willing to take her back to Victoria and let her go where she pleased. Song Fung packed up her things to follow Chu Ngai the next day, thinking that she was going back to where she came from. But the following day, when the train reached Chicago, Chu Ngai told her that he had some friends in that city where they could go and have a wash. The woman was more than willing to follow him. But when Chu Ngai's friend, Wong Se's room was reached, Chu Ngai told Song Fung to stay and hit the pipe while he would go down stairs and talk with a friend. He did go down stairs to talk with a friend and got the money for his "goods," too. The $1,800 was counted out and handed over to him, and then he immediately took the train back to New York. Meantime Song Fung was waiting in the room up stairs and thinking all the time that her master was a long time coming back for her. When night came no Chu Ngai showed up. Poor Song Fung began her weeping anew. When her new master saw that his slave was well secured he told her the truth, that he was her new master, and the successor of her contract. When Song Fung heard the truth of the transaction she wept bitterly. Finally she lost her sight. The Chinamen in Chicago now call her Mang Ngen Por, meaning "Blind Woman."

When Chu Ngai came back to New York with the price of Song Fung it did not take him long to gamble his money away. When he found himself in need of more money he planned to sell his other slave, Lin Fung. But some good Chinaman informed Lin Fung of her master's intentions, and she gathered herself up as soon as possible and stole away from her prison at No. 17 Mott Street, and, finding her way to the Presbyterian Mission, No. 14 University Place, secured shelter and protection. She is still living with Mrs. Huie Kin, who has taught her how to read her a, b, c's and say the Lord's Prayer.

Besides these ventures, eight young slaves, aged respectively 8, 9, 10 and 11 years, have been brought to Chinatown. This lot of slaves was bought in China and brought into New York by different Chinese families for domestic use as house and body servants. The prices paid for them were from $75 to $90 Mexican currency, equivalent to $38 and $45 American gold. They live at Nos. 15, 21 and 43 Mott Street, and are often seen walking through Chinatown with baskets and tin pails.

They carry food from the store or restaurants to their homes. As a rule merchants do not allow their daughters to carry baskets, or even to walk through the public streets. These girls are taught by their masters and mistresses to fancy all sorts of dreadful things that they allege the Christian people practice. They teach them to understand that it is wicked for girls to know how to read and write, and that the Christian people baptize persons with a deadly solution, or hypnotize them. This fantasy is planted in the minds of the young slaves just as American children are taught Mother Goose rhymes. They are not allowed to attend public school; they are not allowed to speak to Christian Chinamen; they are not allowed to know any domestic affairs; and only eat the scraps left by the masters. When they attain the age of 14 or 15 their masters will sell them to the Mott Street merchants for concubines for $800 or $1,000 apiece.

Female slave trade of this nature in New York's Chinatown is becoming to be regarded as one of the most profitable investments. Whenever these children receive an order from their mistress their duty is to obey to the very letter. Otherwise they would be punished with a severe whipping. The poor things dare not tell their situation to anyone in the world. Indeed, they have no friends in whom to confide. Nor do they know that any wrong is being done them. They can only cry in secret when their pains are severe, or they suffer from hunger. And all this in the great city of New York; which sends relief to the suffering in Ireland, India and Cuba by the shipload.

But the passions of the thousands of Chinese in New York are ministered to, as already remarked, by a vast horde of the lowest, the most degraded, most ignorant and vile white women this great metropolis can produce. These women have abandoned themselves wholly to the Chinese, dwelling in Chinatown, adopting its mode of life, eating its food, and drinking its vile liquors in the worst of white resorts, enjoying its body as well as soul-destroying opium pipe, and conforming in all things, save only in dress, to its manners and customs. Although not slaves like the similar grade of Chinese women, they can be anything else than happy. The highbinder has succeeded in getting them under his control, and compels them to pay him a considerable share of their miserable earnings. The blood money is wrung from them through menace of violence or prosecution. They are made submissive through threats of being turned over to the police and sent to Blackwell's Island. They are stuffed continually with stories of the political power of their persecutors as well as of their ability to secure sworn evidence of any charge they may choose to make against them, even to murder. Thus they yield to the demands made upon them through their fears. And when their payments do not satisfy the greed and rapacity of their highbinder masters they are subjected to kicks, cuffs and blows until they willingly give up their last penny and have to go hungry themselves. And all this goes on regularly and continually within call of Christian churches and within sound of Christian missionary establishments.

But all Chinese women, as already stated, are not prostitutes. They all have a money value, and are purchased with money. The wife is purchased no less than the mistress, and is alike subject to the will of her husband in all things. He may even sell her to another, if he so pleases, without offending any Chinese law or code of propriety. It is estimated that there are now thirty-five Chinese women residing in Chinatown besides the girls already spoken of. But three of these women are public prostitutes. The rest are held either as the wives or mistresses of their owners. These women are seldom seen, except by their owners or husbands, for Chinese usage is strict in forbidding them to go upon the streets under any circumstances. If for some special reason one is permitted to visit another's home, she must be taken in a carriage, even though her destination be only a block away.

In Chinatown the people are reticent regarding their women and girls, but the present belle of Mott Street is a handsome girl of fifteen, recently purchased by a New York Chinaman from a member of the Chinese Legation at Washington. The girl is at No. 19 Mott Street, and it is reported that $1,200 was paid for her.

At a neighboring house is a pretty girl of sixteen who, as Chinatown rumor has it, is held for $1,000, as she is very beautiful and attractive. But the usual price for a girl is $700 or $800. They are generally disposed of when fifteen or sixteen years old.

The police, while not doubting the existence of the evil, at least in some degree, look upon the difficulty of getting proof as the principal object in the way of stopping it. "If a Chinaman says a girl is his daughter or niece, how are we to prove it?" said Chief McCullagh. "And how can we legally prove, whatever our belief may be, that the girl was first bought in San Francisco or China, or that she is actually held for sale here?"

Chinamen are very jealous, and the rules for the goverment of their women are very strict. They respect

A CELESTIAL BEAUTY.

women of their own race much more than they do those of white blood, and look upon the Caucasian denizens of their district with contempt. To a certain extent these women are required to conform to the Chinese custom of remaining in doors. They may not appear upon the streets openly, especially in the day time; while at night the necessities of their vile calling keeps them in their rooms. Hence the necessity entailed upon them of having on hand messengers to do their bidding, which calls into service a corps of otherwise idle and worthless boys and young men, known in the vocabulary of Chinatown as Low Gui Gow. Low Gui means a common woman, and Gow a dog. Thus the phrase means "The common woman's dog." Its application is servant, boy or attendant. Thus a Low Gui Gow is merely an attendant upon a common woman. There are about fifty of these Low Gui Gow in Chinatown—white, black and yellow. They live on the street and hang around Nos. 11, 17 and 18 Mott Street and the corner of Pell and Doyers Streets, near which their patrons have their residences. Thirty white boys, fifteen negroes and five Chinese are so employed regularly. These boys, of course, make their living off the women. They have their own peculiar way of conducting their business and "running things," as they term it. They have Chinatown divided up into districts. Each boy is entitled to wait upon so many women who are duly assigned to him. When a woman wants beer all she has to do is to go to the window and shout for her particular attendant. If her Low Gui Gow is not at his post when called the others signal quickly for him. The signal passes all through Chinatown, and in a minute the boy wanted appears. At very late hours these Low Gui Gow stand around the places where

GEORGE PAPE, CHIEF OF THE LOW GUI GOW.

"Hop" (or opium) is sold, waiting for women from other parts of the city who may come to buy the drug. The boys procure it for them and receive tips for the service, the tip running from 5 to 25 cents. The most profitable part of the Low Gui Gow's business is showing strange Chinamen where "pretty Mellican girls" live. For such service the fee is from a quarter to a half dollar.

The picture here presented is that of George Pape, the chief of the Low Gui Gow in Chinatown. He was born in Philadelphia of negro parents and came to New York in 1891. He does not know when he was born, but says he thinks he is about 22 years of age. He is known to the girls whom he serves as Sam, and his companions of Pell Street call him "Yellow." As will be seen from the picture Sam is not a very prepossessing young man, but, in the vernacular of Chuck Connors, "He gets there just the same."

In addition to being chief of the Low Gui Gow, Sam acts as waiter at night in the Chinese restaurant at 16 Pell Street, and receives a salary of from $4 to $5, according as the proprietor feels on pay day.

Sam has never done any other work than that of a Low Gui Gow, and before coming to New York performed the same offices for the girls in the Chinese quarter on Race Street, Philadelphia. He has never been to school and can neither read nor write. The particular territory over which he has the exclusive right to reign includes 11 Mott Street, 11 and 19 Pell and 6 Doyers Streets, in which there are forty prostitutes. He says he has to keep a sharp lookout all the time in order that his territory may not be encroached upon by the others of his class, and also for the police who chase him and the rest of the fraternity out of the district.

Sam says the Low Gui Gow are always fighting among themselves, claiming that their business is being appropriated by each other. For getting a girl a pint of beer he receives five cents, and for buying twenty-five cents worth of opium he receives ten cents. He does a good "business," although he is not growing rich. He is, as before stated, the chief of the band and is typical of the class.

CHAPTER XIII.

HIP SING TONG.

ORGANIZATION OF THE VILLAINS OF CHINATOWN—PROFESSIONAL BLACKMAILERS, DEALERS IN FEMALE SLAVES AND PROTECTORS OF CRIME.

HE "highbinder" is an American designation applied to a class of Chinese immigrants whose business is crime and violence. It must be remembered that Chinese civilization is radically different from American or Christian civilization. The code of morals of the two nations is widely different. To illustrate, the murder of a female child is not looked upon as a serious crime in China, nor as criminal at all by the middle and lower classes of the Chinese. In America human slavery was abolished thirty odd years ago; but to-day the women of China are bought and sold as freely and as commonly as are cattle among us. The marriage tie in China is a very slender and weak chain, sundered on the slightest pretence and with no material ceremony. Here marriage is considered a binding alliance, lasting through life unless set aside by legal formality and for serious cause. So the Chinese come to us impregnated with the ideas of morality and social relations that obtain in their native land and instilled into them in their early education. It is not to be wondered at, then, that they recognize in their communities a class of men who live and fatten on what we call crime. The Chinese highbinder is otherwise what we call a "thug." He is a far worse character than our "plug-ugly," "brigand" or other lawless villain. But still he is permitted to roam at large and practice his unholy vocation among the Chinese without a protest from them. Indeed, he is openly recognized, and his profession, though possibly not considered quite as respectable as the mercantile or mechanical pursuits, is looked upon as perfectly regular and legitimate. No man was ever punished in China for merely cutting the throat of his female offspring, and why should he be here? If women were not openly sold in China, how would Chinamen get wives? Therefore, why may they not be sold here? Were it not for blackmailing in China, how would the mandarins and other officials live and thrive? Hence, why make a fuss about blackmailing in America? Here you have the Chinese logic of the situation. Hence, you will find highbinders openly practicing their calling in Chinatown and in every Chinese community in America.

Here in New York's Chinatown the highbinders are

formally organized under the society name of Hip Sing Tong. The organization is fully recognized by the Mayor of Chinatown and by the Chong Wah Gong Shaw. Indeed, "it is duly incorporated under the laws of the State of New York;" but that is merely a bluff, and is based on misrepresentation and fraud. It has no excuse for existence that would be entertained for one minute by an American court. Its business is simply to protect its members in blackmailing, in levying tribute upon the vile women of Chinatown, in buying and selling women for the purpose of prostitution, and in the commission of all manner of crimes that may be necessary in the prosecution of its nefarious calling, and require its protecting care. It furnishes, for a price, perjured testimony to acquit any apprehended criminal, or to convict any persecuted tradesman. It guards the portals of the Chinese gambler's den for pay, and, when necessary, assumes to blind the eyes of American policemen to the vices of Chinatown. Indeed, it is broadly asserted that through its agency Police Headquarters has more than once been influenced to withhold its hand from crushing the iniquities which prevail in Chinatown. Why should it not be recognized and well paid for such services as these, especially as they are not repugnant to the Chinese standard of morality and virtue?

The Hip Sing Tong differs in no respect from its sister society of San Francisco, which is called Hip Yee Tong, or translated, "The Temple of United Justice." Thus does crime seek to hide itself under a virtuous name, or thus does the morality of the Orient designate the most odious and hated of villains. Thus the more devilish the business the more sanctimonious the name it assumes as a cloak. Both in San Francisco and here it is a secret, oath-bound body, the betrayal of the mysteries of which renders the betrayer liable to death on sight and without benefit of clergy, or any form of trial or conviction. It costs the enormous sum of two dollars to become a member of this delectable society of professional cutthroats and blood-suckers. Any who wish to join may make application at headquarters, No. 34 Bayard Street.

The fan tan industry in Chinatown, of which more extended mention is made in another chapter, is carried on under the protection of the Hip Sing Tong, which exacts heavy tribute from it for its fostering and shielding care. Probably the Fan Tan Syndicate would be forced to pay even heavier tribute should the Hip Sing Tong swing around and assume an attitude of hostility to it. It makes but little difference to these fellows which side of any cause they espouse so long as they make money out of it. To illustrate the character of the men, or fiends, composing the villainous organization, a prominent member and leader was accused some years ago of robbing and murdering a peaceable laundryman. The police were satisfied of his guilt, but his thug companions managed to spirit away the witnesses who would have proved his guilt, and thus he escaped conviction. Soon after he was arrested at Newark, N. J., for robbery. He was tried, convicted and sentenced to seven years' imprisonment. His criminal friends managed to enlist influential sympathy in his behalf, and he was pardoned after serving but eighteen months of his term. He is now practicing his trade of crime among the Chinamen of New York's Chinatown, and is naturally a shining light of the Hip Sing Tong. What his associates and companions must be can be readily inferred.

The Hip Sing Tong has about 450 members, every one of whom is an expert in crime, as understood in this country, and fully eligible to a residence in state's prison or a seat in the chair of electrocution. Yet, as already remarked, they are not looked upon as criminals by the Chinese whose moral ethics differ so widely from those of Western civilization. They go and come among their countrymen with entire freedom, though well known and their nefarious business thoroughly understood. The highbinder dresses well and carries himself with a great show of importance, though sometimes with rather too much swagger. He usually carries his hands in his pockets to convey the impression that he is quite prepared to draw his weapon—yes, and use it, too—on the slightest provocation. The highbinders are organized in every principal city in this country, though under varying names in the different localities. A bond of union exists between them, and members transfer from one to the other as, for any cause, they have occasion to change their residence from one city to another. It is estimated that there are about 3,000 of the guild in the United States at the present time.

In the prosecution of his calling the highbinder is cold-blooded, pitiless and cruel. Human sympathy is as foreign to his composition as can well be conceived. He is ever ready for emergencies, and has no hesitation at shedding blood, or even committing murder, when he fancies that it is required. Tactfully he seeks to avoid trouble with the more respectable members of the Chinese colony, his victims being those usually engaged in pursuits generally known to be unlawful under the laws of the land. The gambling establishments and the houses of prostitution are his most ready fields of operation.

Here he can levy his blackmail with but little questioning, and enforce his demands at the point of his ever-ready pistol, or, if more quiet is desirable, overcome resistance with a hatchet or "fighting-bar," whichever may be most convenient. His fighting when plying his trade among those whom he blackmails endangers no lives but those already beyond the pale. But when the villains fall out among themselves, as they occasionally do, and hostilities are begun on sight as usual, non-participants are quite as liable to be shot as are those engaged in the shooting. The wretches, crazed by their anger and intense hatred of each other, are then utterly reckless of consequences. They send their bullets flying with careless aim and promiscuous results. They have learned the use of the pistol only in recent years and since coming to America, and are not therefore expert with it. Indeed, they even know very little, technically, about it. When a Chinaman buys a pair of boots he selects the largest he can find, because he gets more leather for his money. So in buying a pistol, only those of the largest size suit him; but after size he requires quality, and selects the best. No cheap affair can be sold to a highbinder.

A Colt 6-shooter of 44 or 45 caliber divides with the Smith & Wesson, the Remington and the Merwin and Hulbert his esteem, but all must shoot the cartridge ordinarily used in rifles. As a rule the double action pistols are preferred, for the reason that highbinder shootings are always hurriedly done, so that police interference may be avoided and the fighters get under cover in the labyrinths of Chinatown. The weapons are never bought directly by the men who will use them.

Several gun stores are located almost within the limits of Chinatown. On the Bowery there is a curious "department store" which is partly given up to hardware and firearms. It is a tumble-down shop, presided over by a weazoned old man who remains strictly neutral between the warring highbinders. They can all buy pistols from him, and pawn them at his place when the immediate occasion for their use has passed.

The arms are rarely purchased until a man has been doomed to death or a fight has been decided on. Then some respectable looking Chinaman, perhaps a merchant, visits a gunshop and with the utmost care selects one or more revolvers of the largest size. The pistols are critically examined as to "pull," certainty of action in the cylinders, and the length of the point on the hammer which strikes the primer and discharges the shell. Nearly all of those purchased have long barrrels, 7½ inches, and are arms intended for army and navy use and to be carried in holsters. But the highbinder has no use for a holster. When he takes up the pistol it is to kill some man within a few minutes and mayhap on sight, so he must have his weapon where it can be gripped and put into action instantly. The peculiar dress of the Chinese especially favors the murderous highbinder in concealing the weapon and yet having it under control. The long, flowing sleeves of the outer garment worn on the street by all Chinamen serve a double purpose for the murderous outlaw.

Often the assassin detailed to kill some fancied enemy or opponent straps his revolver to his forearm by a rubber band or other fastening, from which the weapon can be instantly disengaged. The pistol lies along the inner portion of the arm where it can be carried without observation. If one of the Chinatown detectives chances on purpose to brush against the highbinder in passing, nothing is felt of the weapon that is ready for use as soon as the man marked for death appears.

At other times, when waiting around for a street fight to begin, or when walking from the Tong house to some battle ground, the pistol is carried in the waistband of the trousers where it can be quickly reached by lifting the blouse. In cold weather it sometimes becomes necessary under the highbinder code to put a man to death, and then the assassin may take his 6-shooter in his hand and conceal it by turning down his sleeves.

That way of carrying the pistol is considered equally as desirable with the manner also affected in the cold season, when the assassin covers the hands by hiding them in his sleeves, as ladies use a muff. One hand holds the weapon, and when the victim can be stolen upon, the pistol is merely pushed against the cloth and fired through it. No one sees the pistol and it is easy for the murderer to escape in the excitement which always follows a gunfire in Chinatown.

Searching a Chinaman is a matter quite different from going through a man in American dress. Anywhere from five to twelve garments covering the body must be examined, to make sure that no deftly concealed pocket holds a weapon. Sometimes beneath a half a dozen blouses a coat of mail or an armor of quilted paper is found, either being impervious to bullets.

If the desperate Mongols were expert marksmen there might be less objection to their pistol practice on each other, but they are notoriously erratic shots. A few years ago certain shooting galleries were frequented by Chinese, but when a white man one day killed one of them instead of aiming at the regular target the Chinese patronage ceased. Although quite indifferent to death, the Chinese have not yet learned to handle firearms properly. When they hold the pistol at arm's length they nearly always turn the face away at the instant of firing. A highbinder who can remain complacent among the reports of a thousand big firecrackers shrinks from looking through the sights of his pistol until the lead has been sent on its mission of death.

Sometimes the murderers grasp the pistol with both hands, and by using the double action discharge four or five shots in half that number of seconds. A rest across the forearm is a favorite position and one of the most effective, since it permits of something like steady aim, although it is said that the highbinder never keeps his eyes open when the pistol is discharged.

No remedy at law has been effective in preventing resort to arms by the highbinders. Heavy fines as well as imprisonment have been imposed for carrying concealed weapons, and within twenty-four hours a dozen highbinders were fighting with pistols on the street. The rule made by the police officials operates to lessen the danger to pedestrians about Chinatown, because any Chinese arrested at the scene of a shooting will be compelled to defend himself in court as a principal and pay attorney's fee. Heretofore there has been an agreement among the fraternity to settle their grievances outside of courts, but the new law will make such procedure unnecessary, since nothing can be saved by so doing.

The initiation of new members as highbinders is very

INITIATING A HIGHBINDER.

impressive and trying, and is a ceremony that is held sacred. Only a few privileged Americans have ever witnessed it, and one of these, in describing it to the writer, declared it really impressive. The neophyte, as well as all the officials, are dressed in their richest silken robes. The candidate for admission bows before the great joss, which is in the upper room of the society headquarters, and then kneels. A great two-handed Chinese sword, flaming with jewels like Excalibur, is held directly across his throat; another, but smaller sword, is pressed against the nape of his neck. In this position, more critical than the men who play the role of Damocles, the neophyte repeats in a chant the solemn ritual of the society, with the oath that binds him to renounce all earthly ties and pledge his undivided devotion to the work of the organization. This oath is held unusually sacred by the superstitious Chinese, for the society sees to it that anyone who breaks it does not encumber the earth many moons. Lesser infractions of orders or discipline are punished by flogging, the culprit being bound over a curious wooden instrument which looks like a hobby horse, and the blows are administered with a thick bamboo club.

These men are not criminals because of mere love of crime, any more than a man is a surgeon because of a fondness for inflicting pain. It is their chosen profession, and they practice it for the money they may make from it. They are shrewd enough to understand that many of the pursuits of their countrymen, esteemed innocent by them, are unlawful in this country, and may only be carried on surreptitiously. This affords these cold-blooded professional scoundrels their opportunity. Every gambling game of any kind is compelled to pay them tribute under pain of exposure to the police. Every inmate of a house of shame must in like manner pay, lest the evidence be produced to send her to Blackwell's Island. Every opium joint must contribute a liberal share of its receipts, lest its doors be forced open by the guardians of the law, who are as carefully kept away from the submissive places. For the rest, if a quarrel occurs between two men, one of whom is able and willing to pay to have the other put out of the way, the highbinder is ready to undertake the job. Or if anybody has fallen under the disfavor of the law this enterprising freebooter will, for a suitable "fee," provide the evidence to secure his acquittal. Again, when a neighbor has made himself personally obnoxious, the ever-ready highbinder will secure his conviction of any crime that may be trumped up against him in order to secure his removal from the place. In fact, for pay, the highbinder is ready to perpetrate any villainy, from perjury up to murder, and his oath-bound fellows, under pain of death, must protect him should he fall in the meshes of the law in the practice of his unholy vocation. Talk of the Italian Mafia! There has never existed such another organization of desperadoes and villains as the Chinese highbinders; and these maintain their organization and ply their trade more or less openly in every city of the United States which maintains any considerable colony of Chinese.

CHAPTER XIV.

OTHER CHINESE SOCIETIES.

FONDNESS FOR ORGANIZATIONS ILLUSTRATED—SOME TYPICAL MINOR ASSOCIATIONS.

HE Chinese are great believers in organization. Every trade and calling in Chinatown, as already seen, has its organization or union. They also maintain societies for purely social purposes. It would be impossible to notice all these various societies. Several of the more prominent have already been referred to. Others of any considerable importance may be briefly mentioned.

The Len Ye Tong Society is perhaps the most conspicuous of the social or fraternal bodies. This is commonly known as the Chinese Free Masons, though beyond its secretness it has no likeness to the Masonic Order of the Western World. It is also known as the rebellion party, possibly because of its origin in China during the great Taiping Rebellion. However that may be, the Len Ye Tong is said to have not less than 4,000 members in New York alone. Its rooms and headquarters are at No. 12 Pell Street. It has a temple or place of worship of its own in which Quan Gong, the god of strength, is installed, before whom none but members of the society are allowed to make their devotions. Tom Lee, the former Mayor of Chinatown, has been the leading man in New York of this mysterious organization for the past fifteen years.

The On Leon Society is a social organization which confines its membership to the higher class of Chinese residents. It is bitterly opposed to the Hip Sing Tong, or Highbinders' Society, and seeks to encourage and promote good order and becoming respect to the laws of the land and city which gives the Chinamen hospitality and protection. Most of the merchants of Chinatown are members of this meritorious organization. Tom Lee is at the head of it.

The Sue Yep Kong Shaw is an organization of those hailing from the four southern districts of the Province of Kwong Tong. Its purposes are to guard the interests of its members in social and political affairs, as well as in business matters. To this end it exercises some legislative and executive authority, making and enforcing rules and regulations for the conduct of its members. Limited in this respect by the nativity of its members, it exercises similar power to that of the Chong Wah Gong Shaw, though it recognizes and submits to the superior authority of the latter. Thus its members are required to patronize only those coming from the same districts in China as themselves. The society also charges itself with the duty of recovering the bones of its deceased members and returning them to their native land.

Loong Kon Gong Shaw, another of the many associations or societies in Chinatown, is a development of pride of family. China preserves in its form of government much of the old patriarchial system of the ancient Hebrews. This, with the worship of ancestors, as taught by Confucius, naturally strengthens the family tie among these people and promotes family pride. The Four Brotherhood, which the title of this particular society means, when put into plain English, is an outgrowth of this sentiment. The tradition is that some twelve hundred years ago there were four Chinese patriarchs, named respectively Lau, Kwan, Chang and Chew, who lamented the gradual decrease of their progeny and feared the ultimate extinguishment of their family names. They therefore bound themselves each to the other with a solemn oath to form one sacred tribe or family, as the twelve tribes of Israel were combined in the Hebrew nation. Hence the foundation of this society which has maintained its existence to this day, and embodies the descendants of the original Chinese patriarchs named.

The branch maintained in Chinatown is therefore but a subordinate, or possibly, a merely local organization, of those dwelling here, but tracing their common lineage back to the patriarchs mentioned. It has its headquarters at 22 Pell Street, where, besides a meeting room, parlor and offices, it maintains a shrine devoted to the worship of the particular divinity of the combined families. The rooms are decorated in Oriental style, with considerable pretentions to beauty and attractiveness. Every male who bears either of the surnames of the traditional originators of the clan is eligible to membership. It is estimated that there are about 2,000 of them in the states on the Atlantic coast.

CHAPTER XV.

THE OPIUM VICE.

ITS INTRODUCTION AND SPREAD IN NEW YORK—CHINAMEN NOT THE ONLY USERS OF OPIUM, NOR CHINATOWN THE ONLY LOCALITY WHERE IT IS USED—WHAT THE DRUG IS. ITS USE AND EFFECTS.

HEN England forced her Indian product of opium on China against the earnest and energetic protest of the government of China, she committed a crime against humanity, morality and the well-being of the human race which can never be atoned for. The Chinese race took naturally to the drug, and developed the several manners of its use as a minister to idleness, vice, moral degradation, physical and mental prostration, and final death. Its victims throughout the middle kingdom are numbered by the millions, while the impairment of the national vigor and strength in consequence of its very common use is beyond estimation.

The Chinese brought the vile drug and its habitual use with them to the United States. The people of America are quick imitators of the fashions and follies of others, and are as abject slaves to habit as any other class of people on earth. They quickly noted the illusive pleasures to be derived from opium smoking and opium eating and submitted themselves to the tutelage of the Celestial immigrants in its use. The drug is now accomplishing its deadly work in consequence as well among the white population of the land as among the yellow-skinned newcomers.

When the Chinese, in 1875, began migrating in numbers from the Pacific coast to this city they brought with them their opium pots well filled, and the paraphernalia for its use. But while they settled in an isolated locality by themselves, the noxious fumes of their opium pipes pervaded the entire city and rapidly won devotees to its use. And so it happens that to-day we are debarred from pointing a finger at Chinatown and saying: "There that degrading, disgusting and soul-destroying habit of opium smoking is indulged; therefore, we must drive the Chinese out." Opium is smoked to-day in all quarters of the city and by all classes of the community alike.

The number of "hop fiends," as opium smokers are called, is far greater in New York than people have any idea of, and seems to be growing rapidly. It's a disease. When it gets hold of anybody it seems next to impossible to make it let go. There are thousands of our people who use the drug in one form or another, and the station houses and asylums are full of those who have been pulled down by it. Whisky is bad enough, but as to its effects compared to those of opium, all intoxicating liquors amount to nothing, because the use of the drug is easily kept secret until the victim of the habit is practically beyond all advice or help. There is no cure. A certain uptown druggist could, if he would, tell startling tales concerning the use of this terrible drug—tales that would cause the most profound amazement and anxiety. The "joints" of Chinatown are but evidence of the last stages of the disease—the lowest rounds of the ladder of human disgrace.

The working and mechanic class is probably less tinctured with the disease than any other. Why it is so may be a question not easily answered, but opium users are not found in great numbers among skilled mechanics. It may be that men and women who fashion things simultaneously with brain and hand have less craving for opiates. It is the active brain worker and the restless idler —two extremes—who are most prone to fall before the deadly poppy plant. The disease assails men and women alike—the women are the most unfortunate, because harder to detect. Respectable people, who would consider it vulgar to drink in public, and a lasting disgrace to get drunk on liquor anywhere, will go around under the influence of opium all day and retire drunk from its use every night. Happily this is not as yet general, but there are a great many such—so many that nearly everyone knows somebody so affected.

Frequently the habit is the outgrowth of illness—acquired innocently and accidently. If you would look over the prescription book of any drug store you would be astonished to see how widely opium is used by physicians; and the same is true of patent medicines of all kinds. Opium has its legitimate uses, and confined to those uses is a precious boon to mankind; but beyond this it is a subtle fiend, more deadly because insidious, stealing away brains, honor and life. Better have the yellow fever than the opium habit.

Opium eating, so called, and the one most commonly adopted in European countries, is the simplest method of using the drug. There solid opium is eaten and laudanum is drank. In some cases, bodily suffering, the pain of neuralgia or rheumatism, a troublesome cough, distress due to hunger, diarrhoea, etc., furnish the excuse for the first employment of the drug, its use being often continued after the suffering has passed away. In other cases, sleeplessness or mental trouble induces sufferers to fly for relief to this potent narcotic. Sometimes mere curiosity causes a person to make a trial of the drug. If the special purpose for its use be accomplished it is only too likely that recourse to the drug will be had as the remedy whenever there is the slightest recurrence of the pretext for its use.

Opium is obtained from the milky juice of the poppy plant, which is grown in Persia, India, China and, to a small extent, in Egypt. A portion of that produced in India is consumed at home, and the rest, which is a very large quantity, is exported to China and other countries. With the increase of opium cultivation in China its consumption in British India, Burmah and America is also increasing. The vice of opium smoking, which is more injurious than opium eating, has of late been spreading to an alarming extent. Now opium can be found in almost all towns and cities, and upwards of five hundred thousand acres of the best land in India are devoted to its cultivation. In order to encourage and stimulate its production advances of money are made by the government to the growers, as the crop progresses, without interest, and finally the entire crop is purchased by and taken into the government factories at Patna and Ghazipur (both towns of the Bengal presidency). The raw opium is prepared there for use, and especially adapted to the Chinese market. The annual average production is 12,000,000 pounds, which is consumed in India, China, Burmah and America. The government of India, in fact, is the sole manufacturer and wholesale trader in this baneful drug.

It is hardly necessary to enlarge on the deadly properties of the drug. The reader should simply bear in mind that a dose of a few grains is sufficient to kill a strongly built, full-grown man; or a dose of one, or even half a grain, once a day for six months continually, is enough to deprive him of his physical, moral and mental strength and activity, and to degrade him to the level of a beast. A very robust youth is reduced to a mere skeleton after only a few months' use of this powerful poison, and made incapable of earning even his own livelihood. He consequently falls on the charity of his relatives, and failing that, takes to stealing and other crimes. The opium eater or smoker is invariably a pilferer, even if he has money enough of his own to buy the supply he wants. The miseries of the victim are not so painful to us as those of his relations and friends. When the head of a family, or in other words, the breadwinner of a household consisting of wife, helpless children and old and infirm parents, gives himself up to smoking Chandu (compound opium), his home becomes a horrible place, an actual and visible hell on earth. Starvation, want and misery always reign there. However hard-hearted a man may be, he cannot refrain from shedding tears on hearing the piteous cries and seeing the wretched condition of those innocent children, who invariably surround their equally needy mother and ask for food in a weakened and most piteous voice.

The opium eater, as a rule, does not sleep at night, except during the latter part, and consequently spends the greater part of the day in dozing, and the rest in indulging his appetite for the drug. His time is spent in idleness, and his money, if he has any, in buying opium and making Chandu. He is the most filthy creature on earth, and unfit altogether for any human society.

In addition to all these, opium makes him most licentious. In fact there is hardly any defect or weakness which is not habitual with him. Religious sentiment is deadened in him, and religion and morality become matters of ridicule to him. In case of poverty the wretched victim, in order to secure a pipe, is driven to the perpetration of crimes of heinous and horrible kinds, which can be better imagined than described. Time, wealth, energy, self-control, self-respect, honesty, truthfulness, and everything that is honorable in a man, are all sacrificed by him to it. The only thing to be said in his favor is that no one ever heard of one being caught red-handed in a murder, as is the case with many a drunkard and blangee (eater of Indian hemp). But this is due more to his natural cowardice and bodily weakness than to any other cause. He is invariably a coward, utterly unable to defend himself, his wife or his helpless children. Young men and women will sacrifice their last piece of wearing apparel and all earthly belongings, as well as their relatives' articles of value, to obtain the necessary drug. Wives will secretly empty their husbands' purses; sons will rob their mothers; fathers will permit their offspring to starve, all to obtain indulgence in the use of this horrible stuff.

There are nine different forms of indulgence in opium, namely: smoking, gum eating, opium ashes eating, opium pill eating, prepared opium eating, laudanum drinking, morphine eating, the use of morphine solution, and the hypodermic injection of opium.

In 1840 about 20,000 pounds of opium were consumed in the United States; in 1880 the consumption had increased to 533,450 pounds. In 1868 there were about 90,000 opium eaters in the country; now they number over 500,000. More women than men are addicted to the eating of opium. The vice is one so easily acquired, so easily practiced in private, and so difficult of detection, that it presents peculiar temptations and is very insidious. The relief from pain that it gives, and the peculiar exaltation of spirits, easily lead the victim to believe that the use of it is beneficial. Opium and Chloral are to-day the most deadly foes of women.

There are about twenty or more places in Chinatown in which opium is sold in twenty-five and fifty-cent portions, which means about 10 to 16 "fun" (a fun is one candareen). The gum, which is bought from wholesale druggists, is spread out thin in a baking pan and baked slowly over a mild fire until almost crisp. It is then dissolved in water over night and strained through a piece of fine flannel. Then it is again boiled over a slow fire until the liquid becomes of the consistency of molasses. This is known as No. 1 opium. It is not the best No. 1.

The best No. 1 comes from Hong Kong, and is sold in cans on which the government collects a duty of $5 to $6, and costs about $8 for one-half pound. This is known as Fook Yuen, or "Fountain of Happiness," and Li Yuen, or "Fountain of Beauty."

Besides the Fook Yuen and Li Yuen brands, there are four other brands sold in Chinatown, namely: Ti Yuen, Ti Sin, Wing Chong and Quan Kai. These last-named brands come from British Columbia and their quality is about equal. No duty is ever paid on the last-named brands. They are smuggled into the United States by French women, who are employed for the purpose by the Chinese. The manufacturer in Victoria, B. C., makes a shipment to Montreal and then the women take the stuff and carry it over the border to some city or town, such as Burlington, where they leave it until they have sufficient to ship to New York City. The woman who smuggles the drug gets a commission.

CHAPTER XVI.

OPIUM SMOKING.

"HITTING THE PIPE"—THE VICE AS PRACTICED IN CHINATOWN—HOW THE DRUG IS SMOKED, AND THE PLACES WHERE THE HABIT MAY BE INDULGED—THE "LAY OUT" DESCRIBED.

IT HAS already been said that the opium habit is indulged quite largely throughout the city—the vice is by no means confined to the narrow limits of Chinatown. Still, as Chinatown is responsible for the introduction of the awful practice into this community, and as it is more openly, and perhaps more systematically, carried on there, and particularly as it is a prominent feature of daily life in Chinatown, we naturally look there for its practical illustration.

The places where opium smoking is provided for and may be indulged, for a price, by all comers, like liquor-drinking in a saloon, are called "joints." There are a great many of these "joints" scattered throughout Chinatown, the most of them hidden in obscure places, and all more or less surrounded with mystery, out of deference to or fear of the police. For it must be remembered that such places are not countenanced by the law of the land or that of the city.' A description of one of these places will serve as a description for all. To gain an entrance to it you will have to go along a narrow, unlighted, dingy alley to a barricaded door. Upon the signal given by your guide, the door will be open leading through a Chinese wood yard, up a narrow, rickety stairs, along a narrow, creaky porch, to the second flight of stairs leading down to door No. 2. On gaining an entrance there by signal you will find yourself in a dimly lighted underground room where from fifteen to twenty people—Chinamen and white women—will be found "hitting the pipe." Others may be seen sitting at tables gambling away the few pennies they may have.

The place is dark, gloomy and filthy. Along the sides of the apartment are ranged a number of slightly raised platforms, which serve as bunks for the smokers. They are without furniture, save a block of wood, which serves as a head rest or pillow. The paraphernalia or "lay out" for smoking is brought to the bunk on order, by the proprietor or attendant. This "lay out" consists of the following essential articles:

The Yen Tsiang (opium pipe), Ow (opium bowl), Yen Hock (a thin wire used for dipping out the opium and holding it over the light while cooking), Yen Hop (a box containing the opium), Yen Dong (opium lamp), Kiao Tsien (scissors), Sui Pow (a sponge to wipe off the bowl of the pipe when soiled), Dao (a cleaning knife),

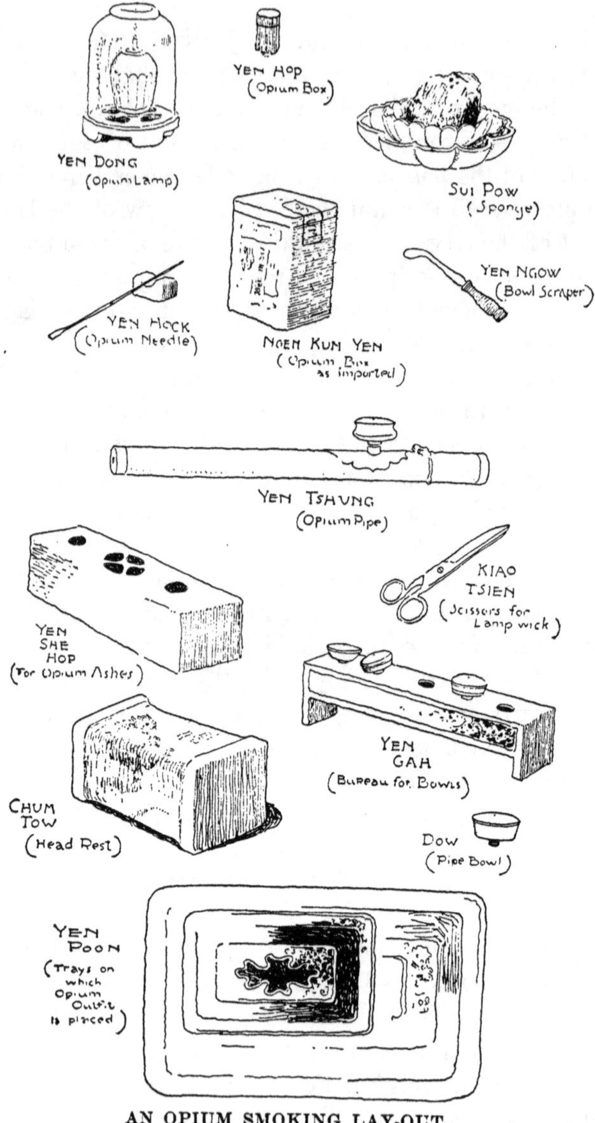

AN OPIUM SMOKING LAY-OUT.

Yen tau Kar (a box or bureau used for setting the bowl on), Yen Shee Hop (a box for keeping the ashes in).

For all this you make payment and are then at liberty to proceed with your smoking, and when satisfied or overcome, sleep and dream as long as you please or can survive in the close, fetid atmosphere of the room.

The person who smokes opium always does so reclining, usually stretched across the hard wooden bunk, which is simply carpeted with straw matting, a small stool or a beveled block of wood serving as a pillow. Resting on his left side, the smoker takes up a little of the treacle-like mass upon the steel needle (yen hock), and, holding it about the flame of a lamp, watches it bubble and swell to six or seven times its usual size. In doing so it loses its inky hue and becomes a bright, golden brown color, giving out a pleasant creamy odor, much admired by old smokers. Poor opium does not yield so pleasant an odor, and is liable to drop from the needle into the flame of the lamp, and rarely gives so handsome a color, the yellow being here and there streaked with black. This process is known as "cooking" the "hop" or opium. Having brought it to a proper consistency, the operator, with a rapid, twirling motion of the fingers holding the long needle, rolls the mass upon the smooth surface of the bowl, submitting it occasionally to the flame, and now and then catching it on the edge of the bowl and pulling it out into strings in order to cook it through and more thoroughly. This is called "chying" the mass or pill.

Rolling it again upon the surface of the bowl until the opium is formed into a small pea-sized mass, with the needle as a center, the needle is thrust into the small hole in the center of the bowl, thus levelling off the bottom of the pea. Then, grasping the stem of the pipe near the bowl in the left hand, the bowl is held across the flame of the lamp to warm it; the bottom of the opium mass or pill is also warmed, and by again thrusting the needle into the small aperture in the center of the bowl and quickly withdrawing it, the mass, with a hole in its center communicating with the hole in the bowl, is firmly fastened upon the surface.

Inclining the body slightly forward, the smoker tips the pipe bowl across the lamp until the opium is just above the flame, when it commences to sizz and bubble. With the lips firmly compressed against the ivory mouthpiece, the devotee inhales strongly and steadily, the smoke of the burning drug passing into his lungs. This smoke, which is returned through the mouth and nose, is heavy and white, and has a not unpleasant, fruity odor. Having finished this pill or polus, which requires but one long or a few short inspirations, the smoker cools the bowl of the pipe with a damp sponge, and repeats the operation of cooking, rolling and smoking as often as is necessary to obtain the desired effect. Smokers are classified as "long draw" and "short draw" men, or as "hop fiends" or "pleasure smokers," according as they consume the mass in one long or a few short inspirations. The "long draw" is unquestionably the most injurious. "Hop fiends" are habitues and "pleasure smokers" novices.

The habitue, after smoking his allowance, which varies from seventy-five grains to two ounces, feels a pleasant sense of exhilaration that merges into a condition of dreamy wakefulness. It is a state in which the devotee finds himself perfectly happy and contented. The squalid surroundings of the opium den, the harrassing cares and trials of life are banished, and an indescribable sense of complete satisfaction takes possession of him. This waking dream, this silken garment of the imagination, will take its shape and coloring from the most cherished and brilliant strands that run through the web and woof of his life's story. It hides the unpleasant conditions of every-day life, and gives birth to a pleasant bubble, the brilliant play of the colors and misty outline of which are born of the pipe alone. As the smoker's hopes, ambitions, aspirations are, so will be the figures and incidents of his opium dolce far niente.

After frequent indulgence the habitue finds that the pleasant things that at first always came at the pipe's bidding now fail to appear, and, disgusted with the pleasureless practice, he tosses aside the pipe in disgust, only to find that at a certain hour the following day he must smoke again; not drawn to it by any fascination, but driven to it by the horrible sufferings that follow close upon the heels of any attempt to abandon it.

The opium pipe, the origin and antiquity of which are unknown, though it is supposed to have first come from Arabia, consists of two parts, a stem and a bowl. The stem is usually of bamboo, one joint and a quarter, or twenty-four inches in length, and four inches in circumference. When new it is of a straw color, but with long smoking becomes black and glossy. It may be of ivory, orange, or briar wood, or sugar cane, and is occasionally made of lemon rind, cut, dried and polished. The lemon stem gives a peculiarly pleasant taste and odor to the smoke.

At about the junction of the middle third, or just back of the joint, a place is hollowed out of the side of the stem and communicates with its longitudinal perforation. About this hollow there fits closely a shield of metal, usually brass, that rises in a rim about the hole. Into this is fitted the bowl. On either side of the stem is fitted a button of ivory. These stems may be plain, or ornamented with silver and gold, and variously carved. The bowl may be bell-shaped, oval or hexagonal. It is usually of hard, red clay and hollow. On its under surface is a neck or flange by which it is fitted into the stem. To make it fit tightly this is wrapped with strips of soft linen.

The upper surface of the bowl is either flat or sloping downward and upward. In its center is an opening about sufficient to admit an ordinary darning needle. The whole pipe is called yen tsieng, or opium pistol.

The Chinese opium smokers prize old pipes very highly, and they are sometimes handed down from father to son as precious legacies. After an old pipe has been buried with the remains of a dead smoker, and when the smoker's bones are disinterred for any purpose, the old pipe is recovered and carefully kept by the existing head of the family. The oldest son only is entitled to use the pipe of his deceased father. There are pipes now in use in Chinatown which are claimed to be upwards of 50 years old. There are also two establishments for repairing pipes, a line of business which is said to yield at least $5,000 a year.

There are many Chinamen in Chinatown who make a living buying Yen Shee, or opium ashes. They collect these ashes from all available sources. This refuse is dissolved in water, when it is subjected to a process by which whatever of the original drug may be retained in it is recovered and manufactured over. This is known as No. 2 opium. It is then mixed with No. 1 and becomes what is called Yen She Kow, or "half and half," and is sold at a reduced price to the lower class of "joints" and to those smokers who cannot command the price of the pure drug. Fortunes, or what are esteemed such among the Chinese, have been made from this business.

---o---

CHAPTER XVII.

IN AN OPIUM DEN.

SCENES AND OBSERVATIONS WITHIN A JOINT IN CHINATOWN AS RELATED BY A VISITOR—THE AVERAGE OF THE DENS OF VICE IN THAT LOCALITY.

A CLEAR conception of the awful degradation, immorality, beastliness and total depravity produced by submission to the opium habit can hardly be obtained from any mere words. Personal observation only can disclose the utter blackness of the picture which has no relief. The following description of scenes within an opium joint in Chinatown is furnished by one who made his visit solely for purposes of observation and study, and to gain a clearer and more intelligent view of the wretched place and its features, and of the miserable wretches who patronize it, than can otherwise be obtained.

"The hands of a clock prominently displayed in the window of a Chatham Square jewelry store point to 2 o'clock in the morning. The boulevard of the East Side is thronged with pedestrians. Night brings them over here when the rest of the city is asleep, recalling the old adage, 'One-half of this great city knows nothing about the other half.' Within half a dozen doors from the shop where the clock hangs is Pell Street, a narrow, dark, gruesome thoroughfare. This portion of the Chinese quarter is given over to the occupancy of loose women and men who are, if anything, on a lower scale, morally, than their wretched consorts. The houses are old and dilapitated, veritable rookeries, swarming in the daytime with Mongol-American children who give place, as night draws near, to the frowsy-haired and foul-mouthed women who make the dark halls a rendezvous. No. 10 is a house much like the rest, with possibly the exception that an air of quiet pervades it in the daytime. Visitors are few, occasionally a man or woman better dressed than those of the neighborhood. They come from the Tenderloin, and in the early part of the night are frequenters of the Empire, the Bijou on Sixth Avenue, the Haymarket, and similar places. They climb up the steps leading from the cellar and hurry away. These steps lead down to a little square bit of standing room, built about with boards nailed firm and strong, as if an attack was expected. Little pencils of light sift through cracks made by inequalities in the timber, and from a knothole in the door a single red eye in the forehead of a very watchful demon confronts you. If you would enter: knock, wait, and presently you will hear the rattle of a chain, the shifting of a bolt and the door is opened by an attendant who peers out into the gloom, bringing with him a smell, pungent and heavy. If he knows you, or concludes that you look all right, the chain is loosened and you enter the opium 'joint.' Near the door is an apartment very much like a booth at a country fair; or like an enclosure in Central Park, where the sacred bull or some other animal is kept to be stared at. In the booth is a platform which takes up nearly all the available space. It is two feet from the floor, and is covered with Chinese matting. In the center is a square black walnut tray holding a variety of articles familiar to the opium smoker. They are the 'lay out.' By the tray is the pipe itself. This particular pipe is a good one and brought on here from San Francisco by Mo Hing. It is used only by the Celestial proprietor. A piece of bamboo about fifteen inches long, so soaked by repeated smokings that it looks like ebony, is the stem. Two-thirds of the distance from the ivory mouthpiece is the bowl, made of red clay and marked around the sides with Chinese characters. The top of the bowl is flat, but in the center is a pin hole over which the cooked pill is placed. This particular pipe is worth $50. The value increases with age. A Chinaman is smoking. He is Sing, the proprietor. His lips are fixed against the mouthpiece, and he draws steadily. While the smoke is ejected through his nostrils the pill makes a crackling noise as it turns over the flame and as it is gradually drawn into the little hole.

"Pass between the folds of a calico curtain to the joint proper and this is what you will see. It is a room about thirty feet long by about twelve wide. Beginning at a point about three feet from the floor are several separate and distinct strata of smoke which rise and fall like the bosom of the sea disturbed by a swell. The pungent odor which greeted you at the door is intensified a hundredfold, and is heavy and sensuous. A score of little lamps dot the place here and there, and are burning bravely, as if they were trying to light up the surroundings. Their attempt at illumination is a failure. They were not intended to illuminate, hence their failure in that regard. Vice loves gloom and goes hand in hand with darkness. Here is vice of the vilest kind—imported vice. On either side of the room there is a row of board bunks, as habitues say, erected about two feet from the floor and covered like the platform in the outer room with matting and dotted with wooden head rests or little wads of straw covered with green gingham, which serve as pillows. This is the hour for the fiends, and there is little unoccupied space on the bunks.

"A party of four is the usual company with one 'lay out' and one pipe. Two lie, one on either side of the tray and use the head rests. The other two lie on their companions, so that no space is wasted. One acts as cook and the pipe goes around in turn between choice bits of conversation and morsels of gossip. 'Hop fiends' do not stand on ceremony nor among them is regard paid to personal appearance while in the joint. There is a knock at the door and a party of newcomers is announced. A handsome girl of about 18 years and her 'man' among them, enter and exchange greetings with the doorkeeper.

"'Hello, Pete! How is graft?'

"'A lay out, Sing,' she says to the Chinaman, 'and hurry up; I've got the yen-yen terrible.' Yen-yen is Chi-

SCENE IN A CHINATOWN "JOINT."

nese for habit—a craving for the pipe. She must smoke to relieve that terrible pain. To stop that tiresome yawning and to bury that feeling of intense depression. The calico curtain is brushed aside and they enter the joint proper. The man is recognized. He is a green-goods man and a successful one, and he receives the attentions paid him with befitting dignity.

" 'Hello, Harry; how did you hit them lately?'

" 'Oh, fairish. Seen McNally?'

" 'Nope! He ain't been here since last night. I heard he went to Philly to right up the guys there.'

" 'Ah!'

"Leisurely, and as if she was alone in her own room, the girl begins to disrobe. It is warm in the joint and she carelessly removes her cloak, hat, dress, corsets and shoes.

" 'Move up a little, can't yer,' she ejaculates impatiently. And when a spot is cleared she lies down while the attendant, Chu, brings in tray and pipe, for which he receives fifty cents. The opium for the common smoker does not come in the hop-toy. A black lump about the size of a silver quarter is stuck on a playing card. The card upon which Nell's dope is placed happens to be the nine of clubs.

" 'Oh, the nine of clubs! Well, well!' and she laughs heartily. 'I'm going on a journey across water.'

"Harry's coat is off and he is preparing to lie down.

" 'Well, you make me tired. Yer worse than an old hag, with all yer signs and things. Cook the hop and don't be cracking so much.' And obediently she begins. With a delicate touch she dips the point of the yen hock into the black, shiny, sticky mass, and after a few twists brings it forth with a round lump about half the size of a pea on the very tip. Nell has been smoking for five years and she can cook like a Chink (Chinaman). As the little lump is held over the flame it begins to simmer and cook, and turns a rich golden color, as it gradually puffs and grows to five times the original size. Tiny jets of smoke spurt forth here and there, as presently she begins to roll it down on the smooth surface of the pipe with marvelous dexterity.

" 'Been here long?' asks Harry of his nearest neighbor.

" 'Yes, since the day before yesterday. But I'm going out to-morrow to get down to graft.' (Graft means stealing of some kind.)

"Nell is heating the pill again, and as it simmers she works it back and forth on the edge of the bowl to get all the poisonous juice out of it.

" 'Yer take a year with that pill,' growls Harry. 'What do yer want to chi it for?' (The kneading process is known by the Chinese word 'Chi.')

"With a quick jerk the pill, rapidly hardening, is removed from the pipe and the rolling goes on until it assumes the shape of a high silk hat without the brim. Then the space about the little pin hole is heated, the bare point of the yen hock is stuck in the aperture and the pill made fast. The steel is withdrawn and it is ready to smoke.

" 'The cook has the first pill,' says Nell, and she has her way. With her lips pressed against the big ivory mouthpiece she draws long and steadily, just as Sing, the Chinaman, did in the other room, and a coil of heavy, aromatic smoke goes up to strengthen the cloud-like wave near the ceiling.

" 'Sing 'Marguerite,' Imogene, will you?' asks Nell of the other woman, as she takes another little black lump from the nine of clubs, and as she rolls it the singer begins softly, and the buzz of conversation is lessened, for Imogene is a professional and can sing 'proper.'

"And thus an hour passes and one is glad to pass out into the fresh air again. But I wanted to have a really novel experience, so I went back there and became one of the 'fiends' for a few hours. Imogene was still singing 'Marguerite,' and as she sang she kept cooking over the little lamp. She was a fine looking girl. Her hair black and glossy, her eyes brilliant, the pupils apparently dilated. She had not been working for two weeks and remarked:

" 'Ever since my last engagement I have lived right down here in this cellar, eating only when absolutely necessary and sleeping away the few hours of early dawn, when the tide in the joint was at its lowest ebb.'

"Two weeks may seem a long time to live down there in the smoke and smell of a crowded room where the Celestial owners cook their meals, but I found a girl over in one of the corner bunks who said she had not seen a ray of daylight for six weeks. She came in with $118 in her pocketbook and she was 'going up against the pipe,' according to the cant term of the joint, for all she was worth.

"Imogene's song has ceased and she is humming a snatch of a Bowery ballad. Four persons enter. They are girls, women, or whatever you please to call them. One was addressed as Italian Rosie, another was known as Dutch Bertha. Two of them are not new to the place, and they salute the doorkeeper with:

" 'Hello, Pete, how are things? Lottie down here to-night?'

" 'Nope,' responds Pete.

" 'It's only Berth; she's going up against it to-night, ain't you, Berth?' and Berth nods her head violently once or twice, as if she was afraid to say anything. There is a difference between her and the rest, but the barrier between them will be broken down as soon as the fascination of the pipe and the pungent smell and the company of congenial companions come upon her. Thenceforth she will look forward only to the time when she can go to the joint. She will forget her other shame in this new one, and will look upon money as representing so many 'shells of dope.' She seems a willing victim, for she has heard from her companions of the pleasures, real or alleged, which follow a smoke.

" 'I say, Rosie,' said Bertha, pausing in the act of removing the last stains of opium from the middle spot of a three of diamonds, 'there's Mamie and Dutch Rose and they've got a new girl. I suppose she is thinking now that she'll go to sleep and be in heaven as soon as she hits it.'

" 'Ah, forget it. They all make me tired,' replies Rose. She is a languid looking blonde woman, and one of the worst victims who smoke. And as she reclines on the shoulder of a one-armed man the light of the lamp shows great dark rings beneath her eyes, and her cheeks sunken. She first smoked ten years ago, and now the one-armed man has all he can do to keep her supplied with the dope. He is a well-known counterfeiter and all-around crook, and is popular because his sister can go into any big department store and lift a bolt of cloth into her capacious pocket without being detected by the house man. He is in the business himself, but is not very successful on big jobs, because he is handicapped by the loss of his arm.

"'Well,' returns Bertha, meditatively, as she finishes cooking the last pill and sticks it on the bowl with a deft motion, 'that's just the same way I walked in here four years ago. Only it wasn't a woman brought me here, it was that Spanish Joe, the Peter Guy, and I wish I'd never seen him. I'll smoke this pill considering it is the last, and considering also that I haven't got the price of another shell.'

"She smokes as slowly as she can, without running the risk of burning the pill, and when the last golden fleck of the drug has disappeared into the little hole which has taken in hundreds of dollars and given out nothing but smoke, she lays the pipe down and continues:

"'When I was first brought up against this thing' (and she lays her hand carelessly on the bamboo stem) 'I thought that as soon as I took a couple of puffs I would be dead to the world. I thought hitting the pipe was a terrible thing. But Spanish Joe, and everybody else, for that matter, said it wouldn't hurt a baby, and I went at it.'

"'But a good many think,' interrupted Rose, 'that it will make you unconscious as soon as you hit it.'

"'So they do. And that's the idea that I had. When Spanish Joe cooked the first pill for me I was afraid as death. But they all got around me and said: 'Go ahead, Bertha; it won't hurt you,' and it didn't hurt me at all. The smoke wasn't half so bad or strong as cigarette smoke, and it didn't choke me when I swallowed a little bit. I smoked for three hours that night, and I was so sick I thought I would die. I was so dizzy that I fell on the floor right in between the bunks here. They poured water over me and everything else they could think of. The first thing I remember was when I opened my eyes and found my face all wet. Of course if I had kept quiet while smoking, instead of getting up and running around between each pill, I'd have been all right. And then I smoked a whole lot for the first time; in fact, too much. I didn't see anything so nice about it. I liked the smell when I was smoking. Smells something like peanuts roasting.'

"'Yes, a little bit.'

"'I got in the way of coming down here because all the rest of the people came down here. And every night after the show—I was working in Miner's then— I used to put for the joint and stick away into the morning. That was when I had the company habit and liked to come here just for a chance to talk with the boys. Ah! but when I learned to cook; my, wasn't I proud? I wanted to be cooking all the time, just for the sake of cooking. Well, it didn't take me long to get the habit after that. Then the yen-yen came and I used to have to smoke to keep from getting sick. Now I suppose I'm up against it for good.'

"'Well, what's the difference anyhow?' said Bertha. 'You can't die but once, and you might as well die in front of a shell of dope as any other way. Hide your face up, Rose, here comes the ward guy with a crowd. I don't want to be stared at, for my part.'

"The ward man just enters with a slumming party. Four well-dressed men and one woman, chaperoned by the officer. This is not at all an unusual event, and hardly a day or night passes without the advent of one or two of these parties. When the sightseers had left, Bertha's load of hop proved too much for her and she fell asleep, while the vigilant and economical lookout, Pete, came clattering in and took away the pipe and tray. It was almost dawn now, and the buzz of conversation had gradually died away, and the little fairy lamps had been extinguished one by one, while there remained only one or two here and there, flickering away like philanthropic fire-flies trying to penetrate the darkness—darkness of the cellar which so charitably threw a mantle of gloom over the debauchees and hid from view the too scantily clad women who were, for the time being, happily unconscious of their wretchedness."

A HOP FIEND'S DREAM.

A hop fiend went on a weary stroll,
In search of a friend who a pill could roll.
He had not smoked for a whole long day—
He was "barred" from the joints—for he could not pay.

He strolled along with a yen-yen bad,
Till he found a guy who some money had;
He touched him quick and off he flew
To "cop" the hop from the Chink's bamboo.

He smoked, and smoked, and smoked away,
And thought of the riches he'd have some day.
He thought of his friends and roasted all;
For a fiend who won't roast, is no fiend at all.

He finally into a sweet dream fell,
And dreamed of everything—all but Hell.
He dreamed sweet dreams of untold wealth,
And of all the dough he could cop by stealth.

He dreamed of diamonds and riches rare,
And of all the suckers he could ensnare.
He was worth a million in nickels and dimes,
And counted them over a thousand times.

He owned houses and lots, cattle and sheep,
And a million ships that sailed on the deep.
He was king of the world, whom all obeyed,
And was in the most gorgeous garb arrayed.

He had a thousand wives, so pretty and rare,
All dressed in the finest, with golden hair.
He'd a billion servants, who stood at his call—
For Aladdin's palace wasn't in it at all.

He kept on dreaming, until he awoke,
Only to find he had run out of dope.
"Yen Shee Gow."

CHAPTER XVIII.

A TENDERLOIN JOINT.

WHERE "MELLICAN" MEN AND WOMEN PRACTICE THE VICE —MORE PRETENTIOUS APARTMENTS, BUT THE SAME WRETCHEDNESS—GAMBLERS AND THIEVES, WOMEN AND BOYS MIXED TOGETHER LIKE BAIT IN A BOX.

HAVING seen the vice of opium smoking in the depths of Chinatown, where it is indulged by the Chinese and their miserable victims of the lowest strata of white society, it will be interesting and instructive to take a look into an uptown joint, from which Chinamen are excluded, and where only the white graduates of their horrible teachings are permitted to enter and pursue their downward way. For this purpose one of the most pretentious of the many scattered throughout the city is selected.

A house on West Forty-sixth Street, near Seventh Avenue, enjoys the distinction of having been at one time the most luxuriously furnished joint, not only in New York, but in the United States. In the first place, it was not a mere flat, like some of the better classes of opium dives that exist in the city, nor was it a mere room over a stable as are some others. It was like none of these, but occupied the entire house, from garret to basement, and was in a respectable street, having the further advantage of being practically next door to a very much frequented part of Broadway.

Harry A. Hamburger and "Sammy" Goldstein, alias Wood, were the proprietors. Hamburger himself was the McAllister of opium society. He did not himself indulge in the seductive drug from the sale of which he got his income. He merely contributed his genial presence to those who gave him their money for the privilege of transforming themselves into wallowing brutes and chattering idiots in his house.

There was nothing in particular to attract your attention to the house as you approached it in the shade of night. Perhaps the bright light in the basement glass door, while all the rest of the house was wrapped in gloom, was a little unusual and suspicious. Yet it would hardly have aroused curiosity in the ordinary belated pedestrian. The shutters of the house, particularly those of the front parlor windows, were always fast closed, and behind them and the windows heavy curtains fell. Not a ray of daylight straggled into the rooms, and not a ray of the dim gas and lamp light within escaped to the street. All was very dark, solemn and silent.

Your guide knew the way. You merely pressed the electric button at the door and he did the rest. There was first the clamor of the distant muffled bell, and then footsteps were heard clumping down a flight of stairs. It was not a pleasant face that presented itself at the window and looked at you with keen, suspicious eyes. It was not the face of a man you would clasp to your bosom with hooks of steel. To dispose of this branch of the subject at the outset, it may be said, not to put too fine a point to it, that the face of the chief philanthropist, as well as that of any one of his more attractive assistant philanthropists, would send a chill of horror through the forecastle of an Algerian pirate.

When the formalities of inspection had been gone through with, and you had for an instant exposed your back to the blood-freezing bandit at the door without having a knife plunged into your vitals, you had only to follow him up a narrow flight or stairs to the first floor of the house, and there you were.

It was a very simply constructed house. There was a front and back parlor, and between these two rooms was a narrow strip of a room, a sort of long, closet-like recess, about six feet wide. In this recess, and to the right as you passed from the back parlor into the front, was a handsome upright piano. Double doors, which had been taken from the hinges, faced each other opening from the recess, and so formed an unobstructed passageway between the two parlors. The piano fitted snugly in the recess, and was flush with the sides of the doors to each room, so that the player, as he sat on his stool, was in the passageway between the front and back parlors.

Double doors once opened from the front parlor into the hallway at the side, but they were closed up, and in the parlor were covered by a heavy portierre which wholly concealed them. Portierres were a great feature of adornment of the two rooms. They covered every door and hung from every conceivable place from which a person, with a passion for portierres, might hang them. Large and heavily framed pictures, steel engravings of not a bad order, adorned the walls in both rooms, and the windows of the front and rear parlors were covered with lace curtains, surmounted by lambrequins.

The furniture of the rooms was very simple—there wasn't any. Not a chair or table was to be seen. In place of them, and scattered along the floor of both rooms, were strips of straw matting dyed a deep scarlet. Between the matting and the thick carpet which covered the floor, well stuffed mattresses were comfortably placed. At intervals along the walls and on the matting were placed hard, carpet covered ottomans, which were used for head rests.

All of this, it is to be understood, you are very far from taking in at the first glance. As you entered the room, coming from the lighted hallway, you could only see, by the light of the tiny lamps and from jets turned down low, the dim outlines of things like shadows in the gloom. As your eyes became accustomed to the darkness, the huddled lumps on the matting took human form with ghastly white faces, which seemed almost phosphorescent in the faint glow of the opium lamps which fell upon them. Yes, there they were, men and women, and hollow-eyed, cadaverous wrecks of mere boys, tan-

SCENE IN A WEST FORTY-SIXTH STREET "JOINT."

gled together in mixed groups about each lamp—outstretched, outdrawn, ghastly faces resting on their arms in the deep drugged opium sleep. The stench of cigarettes filled the rooms, and with it came the pungent odor of the sizzling opium as it spluttered over the lamps, while the smoker drew its poisonous inhalations from the pipe stem deep down into his lungs.

The floor in both rooms was so thickly strewn with men and women that you could with difficulty make your way through the tangled feet and legs. Wallowing is the predominant posture of the opium smoker. A couch of any kind seems to be beyond his ambition. Just let him get prone on the floor, and there let him grovel on one common level of sodden debauchery with the best—if there be any—and the worst of his fellow wretches. That is all he wants—that is his paradise.

Among the customers at the West Forty-sixth Street joint were both men and women whose faces were well known to the public. For the accommodation of such as these, and for other parties of half a dozen or more who wished a certain privacy, there were two rooms rather luxuriously furnished on the second floor of the house. Both these rooms and the two parlors on the first floor were nearly always filled. The more cautious class of smokers, particularly the women, came in the daytime and early evening, the women wearing long veils very often.

The midnight and the early hours past midnight were generally chosen by the regular element. Bunco steerers and the more prosperous grade of fallen women, very often expensively and not untastefully dressed, were among these. Here and there, out of the gloom of the darkness that pervaded the place, diamonds flashed in the dim light of the little lamps on the floor. A very popular resort with the green-goods brand of swindlers was this place, and it was said that Jim McNally, now in State's Prison in Illinois, who is an eminent member of that fraternity, was backing the place with his cash.

The scene was pretty nearly the same every night, and every night the customers were pretty nearly the same. On one particular night there was a low murmur of conversation floating above the heads of the incumbent groups, which, however, was not unusual. You could hear what was said if you wished, but one circle seldom heeded another. Now and then a cracked, bedrugged voice raised a quavering song, in which others joined in an irregular, mumbling way, as if trying to appear happy. Then some one attacked the piano, and some one who really could sing joined in. That sweet old song beginning, "These words no Shakespeare wrote, these lines no Byron penned," which was such a favorite with the late unfortunate Prince of Austria, was sung with plaintive earnestness by a forlorn creature in purple and fine linen, whose face was a ghastly, waxy hue, and whose eyes had the glistening feverish lustre of the consumptive. But the song did not meet with general approval.

"Now, how's a man to keep his load on with all that caterwauling going on?" came in a querulous growl from a great mass of blubber and sensual selfishness which was having a good bestial wallow all by itself near the middle of the room. It was Joe Blake, alias "Papa Joe," a jewelry fakir and green-goods man.

"Yes," chimed in another voice, "and a two-dollar-and-a-half load at that."

Then there was a dull croaking sound all over the

room which took the place which laughter occupies out in the free air.

In the meantime a man over on another stretch of matting was telling between pipes all about how he got cured of the opium smoking habit at the Keeley Institute.

"It's a wonderful thing," he said, "wonderful. Keeley made a million and a quarter of dollars out of it in one year," and then the cured one hit another pipe.

In the meantime one of the domestic brigands was wandering about among the groups distributing his cards with dabs of opium on them, for which he charged fifty cents each. He distributed drinks, too; but when criticized for awkwardness, he said, with resonant pride:

"I ain't barkeeper, see! Cheese; let go!"

Thus the intercourse went on until dawn came, pale and grey out of the East.

"Be careful of the steps," said little Sheeny Sammy, an attendant, as he let his visitors out of the front door. It was not that he was sentimental about it, but it made a bad mess for a man to break his neck on the steps of an opium joint.

THE LAY OF A LOTUS EATER.

Oh, wicked little dope pill,
  You sphere of poppy dough—
Tho' sin too oft indulged in—
  I fonder of you grow.

Thou dear, diverting hop pill,
  That makes all care forgot;
Without you what would life be?
  A drear and tasteless lot.

The Tenderloin girls all love you,
  You are their heart's delight;
The sight of you brings sunshine;
  Your absence—darkest night.

A DEVOTEE.

CHAPTER XIX.

TOBACCO SMOKING.

THE CHINESE ARE INVETERATE SMOKERS OF THE WEED—THE QUEER PIPES THEY USE—THEY SMOKE BUT LITTLE AT A TIME, BUT OFTEN.

THE Chinese are inveterate smokers, though not all, by any means, are opium smokers. With the really better class the opium habit is considered quite as revolting and injurious as it is by white people. And, indeed, it is questionable if any of the Orientals give themselves up so absolutely to the influence of the drug as do those white people who indulge in its use. A Chinaman who smokes it at all seems, as a rule, to be satisfied with an occasional mod-

SMOKING A WATER PIPE.

erate indulgence, rarely allowing it to become an overpowering or masterful passion with him, as with so many of his Western imitators.

But nearly all Chinamen smoke tobacco, and smoke it excessively. Sometimes they indulge in the luxury of a cigar, but more commonly the pipe is their choice. Their pipes are of peculiar form, which leads the uninitiated to suppose them to be opium pipes. But opium is never smoked by Chinamen or others when standing or engaged in business or work. It can only be smoked while being held in a blaze of fire. The little-bowled, long-stemmed pipes so often seen in use by these people are merely their more popular form of tobacco pipes known as a Souey-kun. The bamboo stem is long and quite large, usually tipped with an ivory mouthpiece. The bowl is quite small, seeming to be infinitesimal in proportion. It holds but a small pinch of fine cut tobacco, barely sufficient for two or three good whiffs. That suffices the industrious man, though he wants his whiffs often.

The more leisurely Chinaman indulges in what he terms a "water smoke"—that is, in smoking through water. For this form of smoking they have several kinds of pipes, as the Sheuy-Yen-Tong, which is a large, slightly curved bamboo contrivance, which is filled with water, the pipe bowl being adjusted near the lower end. There is no mouthpiece to this pipe, its large aperture being pressed against the lips, when, by a strong inhalation, the smoke is drawn from the pipe proper, through the water into the mouth. Another style is called Sheuy-Yen-Tai, and is quite an elaborate affair made of German silver. The water is contained in a small reservoir of any desired shape. Attached to this is the pipe bowl

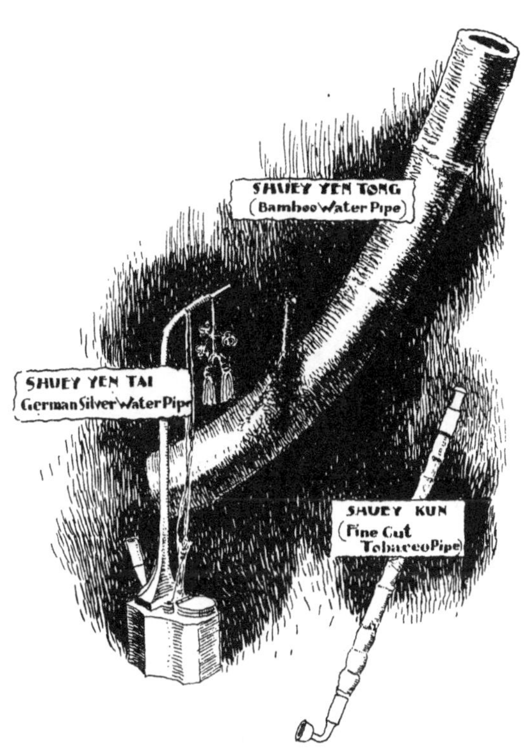

CURIOUS TOBACCO PIPES.

for the tobacco. The stem of silver is attached to the upper part of the water box or reservoir and is bent at its upper end.

In any of these forms John enjoys his smoke hugely, though he can only indulge in his water smoke when at leisure. But in any form the amount of tobacco smoked at one time is very small; though the frequency of his indulgence makes up for the less amount consumed at one time.

CHAPTER XX.

JOHN BEFORE THE CAMERA.

HIS SUSPICIOUS NATURE DISPLAYED—STRIKING A BARGAIN—HUMOROUS INCIDENTS ILLUSTRATIVE OF HIS CHARACTER—BUT HE PAYS THE PRICE AT LAST.

T WILL be found an agreeable change to turn from the vices with which Chinatown is associated to some of the more amusing features of Chinese life. Mr. William A. Ettling, a well-known photographer, who has done much work for these funny people, contributes an interesting and amusing sketch of the Chinaman's antics in having his picture taken. And first as to the suspicion he manifests on entering a gallery.

"When a Chinaman thinks of having his picture taken," said Mr. Ettling, "he drops only casually into the photographer's while out on his regular errands of marketing, bearing a huge bamboo basket on his arm, and a faded umbrella over his shoulder. John cautiously opens the door, and I hear him stealthily creeping up the stairs, till I see his wily eyes peeping around a corner of the hall. After finding out that I have observed him, he comes out of the ante room, leaving in the middle of the floor his various belongings, and turning around on his clumsy feet, once, twice, three times, until his eyes have taken in the entire length, breadth and depth of the studio. It is a comical sight as I see him amble from chair to chair and from one door to another, looking high and low as if he expected to be suddenly surprised by some uncanny spectacle. Hiding his arms within the mysterious recesses of his curious coat, he examines everything, glancing under the table, behind chairs, toward the door of my dark room and stands there tip-toed, as if apprehending the vision of a chamber of horrors.

"Up to this time not a word of recognition has passed between my visitor and myself, as the wise photographer knows if he approaches John at this stage he will surely scare him off the premises, for he is very suspicious as well as superstitious.

"Being assured of his safety, the Celestial is ready for business, and in that the national characteristic of squeezing down the price of everything desired will be observed. But first he makes a very deliberate tour of inspection, examining every picture exposed to view. At last he breaks the suspense by beckoning to me and pointing to a picture hanging on the wall, which he pulls out of its position and reverses to see its back as well as the face. 'How muchee costee dlat?' he suddenly shouts out.

"On being informed that the price is $10 he drops the frame and ejaculates wildly: 'Too muchee! Too muchee! You chargee too muchee money!'

"And thence he goes to another and says less hopefully: 'How muchee costee dlat one?' I tell him six dollars. And he goes the entire circuit of the gallery, winding up at the show case where he looks long and wonderingly.

"John has plenty of time at his disposal, if I haven't at mine, and it takes patience to make a sale to him. Finally he asks of cabinets: 'How muchee you chargee?' 'Three dollars, John,' I tell him. 'Tlee dollars! Tlee dollars! Too muchee money. I give you two dollar,' he says. I say: 'No, John, I charge you three dollars.' John, apparently despondent, edges away from the case to the outer room, where he hastily scrambles up his basket and the numerous parcels with which he is usually burdened, and, without further adieu, steals away, and my time and pains are wasted, you will say. But not so; for about three days afterwards in he comes again, this time with more resolute step and more determined in purpose, and ambles right up to my album and says: 'H'low, Charlie; how muchee you chargee?' He thinks that by this time I have forgotten my former price list, and when I say three dollars he looks quite surprised. I notice him fumbling with a paper bag which he carries with him on this occasion. It contains his black silk cap. His head looks freshly shaven, his face oily and his long black hair neatly braided into his racial appendage.

"John asks: 'You makee good?' and I assure him I

make everything good. There is no hesitation this time, for he immediately adjusts his cap and puts on a delectable grin, and by this time I understand he is ready to be photographed.

"I write down his name, Ling Sing, phonetically, as he supposes I know how to keep memoranda as well as he does with Mellican man's laundry. He gives no address, and rarely, indeed, is he willing to pay anything as a deposit on his pictures. John asks me to write the date for him to call for them, as the Chinese do not expect to see proofs, as they have no idea of the process of photography."

Now they proceed to the operating room where the Chinaman selects the accessories of the picture and gives his instructions regarding the disposition of them.

"I pose him carefully and then retire behind the camera box," continues the narrator, "after bidding him keep his eyes fastened on a certain object which I point out to him. But John don't intend to be fooled by me in this way. He has come to have his picture taken, and his idea of it is that unless he looks right into the opening of the lens he will not be photographed. It is amusing to see him rolling his eyes in a frantic effort to look at the lens, while his position holds him very strained and uncomfortable.

"After making several vain attempts to take him unawares, I finally call out to him, 'Ho-kin-quoy,' which he understands in Chinese to mean 'Look here.' He is very startled at my command of his native tongue, and immediately I get him in the required position. Only now I observe that he has dropped his jaw so that his large white teeth are very prominent, a notion he has that he looks pleasant this way. Again resorting to Chinese I say, 'Hop-ma-go-gow,' which directs him to close his mouth. I make the exposure which, being instantaneous, perplexes John, who had resigned himself to sit patiently for several hours. It takes some persuasion to make him believe I am done."

CHAPTER XXI.

SUNDRY OBSERVATIONS.

BUSINESS INTEGRITY OF THE CHINESE—OFFICIAL TESTIMONY REGARDING THEM—LESS CRIME IN CHINATOWN NOW THAN WHEN IT WAS NOT ONE QUARTER SO POPULOUS—CHINESE OATHS—MANNER OF ADMINISTERING THEM.

ROM the foregoing kaleidoscopic sketches it might be supposed that all Chinamen are worthless characters, given over to licentiousness and vice, and utterly undeserving of any respect or confidence. But that would be an entirely mistaken and unjust judgment. It must always be kept in mind that standards of morality vary. Throughout the Orient, in China no more than in other countries, women are held in absolute subjection to the men, and are esteemed inferior beings, and their purchase and sale is recognized as lawful. Nor is China the only nation which gives official protection to gambling. It is no more lawless for the Chinaman to risk his money at fan-tan than for the American or European tourist to invest in the chance of rouge et noir at Monaco. Let us be just to our Mongolian immigrants. There may be, and undoubtedly are, many bad, vicious men among them, and the moral standard of all of them is quite below our boasted civilization and the teachings of the Christian religion. But the majority of them, despite their strange notions of life and its pleasures, are quiet, peaceable, industrious, sober and strictly honest men. The average Chinaman's word is as good as his bond, and often much better than his oath. Besides being truthful, he is trustworthy. He pay his debts—must do so whether or no. The rules of Chinatown—and of all Chinatowns in the United States as well—make this compulsory upon them. Thus they are rooted and grounded in the fundamental principle of business integrity, which covers a multitude of sins. And this principle, so thoroughly instilled into them from their youth up, naturally produces the fruit of honesty in all their dealings. It would be pronounced absolutely unjust to judge the Anglo-Saxon race by the criminals who occupy their jails and penitentiaries. Equally would it be unfair to denounce all Chinamen as culprits because there are some very bad men among them. The deeds of these criminal ones are rehearsed in our newspapers, and attract public attention and remark, while the quiet, monotonous life of the orderly, industrious majority passes unnoticed. Thus the impression is apt to obtain that the Chinese, as a race, are vicious and lawless. The injustice of this is readily shown, and by the most competent authority—the police who are appointed to look after them.

Patrolman Michael Kehoe is one of the best known figures in New York's Chinatown. There isn't an inhabitant in that queer little section whom he does not know. He has been a member of the Metropolitan police force for the last seventeen years, and since his appointment has been attached to the Elizabeth Street Station continuously, excepting the first six months of his time, when he served for three months in the Eighth Precinct under the late Captain Charles McDonald, better known as "Lightning Charley," and three months under Captain Robert O. Webb of the Seventh Precinct, now retired. Thus he has had a long and intimate acquaintance with Chinatown and the Chinese.

Mr. Kehoe was born in Liberty, Sullivan County, N. Y., March 17, 1860, and was appointed as a patrolman in 1881. He is a model policeman. He has participated in many raids in Chinatown, particularly those made by Inspector Nicholas Brooks, who was then captain, and who made more raids than any other captain who has occupied the position of commander of that precinct. In one of his famous raids more than one hundred prisoners were taken.

Kehoe has also served under Captain Berkholtz, now re tired; Ex-Chief John McCullagh, the late Alexander Wartz, Robert Young, Jeremiah Petty, and Sergeant Reilly, who was Acting Captain for a time, and Captain Dean, who is the present commander of the precinct.

Mr. Kehoe remembers when there were only American business and manufacturing houses on both sides of Pell Street, which is now practically occupied by Chinese in its entirety. The most serious trouble he has had

PATROLMAN MICHAEL KEHOE.

with the Chinese, was on one occasion when a play was given in the Chinese Opera House which reflected on the Chin family, to which the Chins decided to put a stop. They visited the theater in a body, turned out the gas, broke chairs, using the legs of the same as clubs, and continued rioting until the police appeared on the scene. Kehoe arrested the chief offenders and on his evidence they were convicted. He says there is less crime in Chinatown now than there was ten years ago when there were not a quarter so many Chinamen here, and points to the fact that he has only had to arrest two Chinamen within the last six months, and they were only drunk and disorderly cases.

What more need be said in that regard? There are many people who assume to discredit the testimony that may be given in a court by a Chinese witness. This sentiment is an outgrowth of the inconsiderate raid of the San Francisco sand lots upon all Chinamen indiscriminately.

Time and again have counsel asked in the courts of this city that Mongolian witnesses be sworn according to the custom of their country. The request has always caused amusement. The average Chinaman certainly has no regard for the oath taken on the Bible, as he has no more respect for the sacred scriptures than for a spelling book. Hence, unless the Chinese method of swearing is adopted, he usually testifies just as he pleases, with a childlike and bland disregard for the solemnity of the oath. He may tell the truth, just the same, but the oath has nothing to do with it. The Chinese ritual in swearing is very simple. When the witness is called a sharp knife is given him. He grasps it in his right hand and with his left holds a live chicken. Then he cuts off the chicken's head. Next he takes the oath written on paper in his own language, which he burns with incense, and then he is ready. He must tell all he knows about the matter at issue, and must make no mental reservations and must be perfectly impartial. If he does all this he understands that he and his family will be forever blessed. If he commits perjury he believes he will be devoured by tigers, drowned, and suffer untold agony and pain.

By this method of swearing the witnesses justice will be made sure in any case in which a Chinaman is connected; when sworn in any other manner he would have no hesitation in disregarding the truth.

There are other forms of oaths among the Chinese, in one of which the complaint in the case and all the particulars pertaining to it are brought into the Joss House, and then the witness kneels before Joss and, placing his hand on the god's head, says:

"If the statement I am about to make in this case is untrue I am to be punished with every description of torment and agony and die a devil without a head, with no earth in which to bury my body, and these things are to be followed on my generations to come."

Another form in which the same punishments are asked to be visited upon the head of the witness if he swears falsely, is practically the same as the one just recited, with the exception that instead of placing his hand on Joss' head, the witness breaks a piece of new china and spills a basin of water on the earth.

The Chinese regard these oaths as sacred and second to none but the cutting off of the chicken's head.

CHAPTER XXII.

THE CHINESE NEW YEAR.

THE GREAT FESTIVAL OF THE YEAR—THE TIME FOR SETTLING ACCOUNTS AND BEGINNING ANEW—OBSERVANCE OF THE OCCASION—ITS CONTINUANCE TWENTY DAYS.

THE Chinese New Year is a season not merely of festivity among the Chinese, but of business importance. It is not, as with Western nations, a fixed date, but varies as do the Christian festivals of Easter and the days dependent upon it. The Chinese divide their year into twelve months, but their months contain but twenty-nine and thirty days each. The first month is called T'sou, meaning the north corner. Their year begins with the third month of the solar year. An intercalary month is introduced about once in every thirty months, which causes a variance in the first day of the year. New Year's day ranges from the middle of our January to the latter part of February, but whenever it occurs it is the occasion for national rejoicing, individual merry-making and social pleasures. In China all public offices are closed for a period of thirty days, and in like manner the doors of warehouses and shops are shut against customers.

A day or two before the close of the old year a thanksgiving service is held in each household, before the shrine of the tutelary deity, in acknowledgment of the safety and comfort enjoyed during the past year; and, among traders of all kinds, extreme anxiety is manifested to collect outstanding debts, and to provide money for the sums that may be owing. To be a defaulter on New Year's day is to lose credit and reputation, and, rather than begin the new year under such ill-omened circumstances, shopkeepers often offer their stocks in trade at prices far below cost to realize the necessary money. The last night of the year is devoted to cleaning up and preparing for the morrow.

The Chinese in this country, owing to the circumstances by which they are surrounded, and the business methods that prevail here, are compelled to modify their observance of this festival, which they do by curtailing its duration to about ten days. But in other respects they conform pretty rigidly to the customs of their native land. Indeed, in some respects they go further. Thus in Chinatown the matter of debt paying on that occasion is made compulsory, and is enforced by all the power the government of the community is able to exert. This is probably due to the fact that the dwellers here are mere birds of passage, coming from all quarters of the great home empire, whose business relations here are considered at best but temporary. They are not therefore entitled to the consideration they might expect at home and among their own family connections and friends. Therefore the screws are put on rigidly, and everybody is required to make full settlement and begin the new year with a clean account book.

Before daybreak on New Year's morning the members of each household offer sacrifices, with many genuflections and prayers, to Leaven and earth, and to their tutelary gods. After each service firecrackers are exploded in the streets, making the vicinity resemble a dozen old-fashioned Fourth of Julys, boiled down into one. After the tutelary gods have been honored, the deceased ancestors of the household, and after them the living elders of the family receive homage from the kinsfolk. After these sacrifices and ceremonies have been duly performed the male members of the house go out to pay complimentary visits to their friends. A more than usual cordiality is required of acquaintances when meeting in the street, and an invariable law of custom makes it obligatory for everyone to appear in his best attire.

The fundamental idea compelling this observance of the New Year, is that with the new year a fresh lease of life begins. The accounts of all the thoughts, words and deeds of the past has to be closed, and a new era breaks with the dawn. The idea pervades the entire race, from the head to the lowest member. Thus on the occasion of a new Emperor his reign counts only from the first day of the year following the decease of his predecessor, and on each succeeding New Year's day he is re-enthroned, amid a display of royal insignia and the strains of music. He then prostrates himself before heaven and earth, and receives the congratulations of his ministers and the members of his household, as on the occasion of his first accession to the throne. So also the very boys in the street shout "Mai saou!"—"I will sell my idle ways," implying a beginning of a life of industry and usefulness.

The entire first week of the new year, both in China and in Chinatown, is spent in paying visits, exchanging presents and feasting, and the streets are thronged with servants carrying sweetmeats and cakes from house to house. From superiors to inferiors presents of a more substantial value pass, and considerable sums of money are bestowed by the wealthy on their servants and dependants. Beggars reap a rich harvest at the houses of the rich.

While these festivals are extended in China over a period of twenty days, here they last but about a week, our Oriental immigrants having imbibed so much of Western sense as to comprehend that life is not for mere merry-making and pleasure. At the end of the week's indulgence business activity is resumed, under new contracts and with fresh accounts.

According to an ancient tradition current in the northern provinces of China, New Year's day is called the fowl's day; the second, the dog's day; the third, the pig's day; the fourth, the sheep's day; the fifth, the cow's day; the sixth, the horse's day; the seventh, man's day. During the first six days the flesh of all these animals to whom the days are dedicated are forbidden as food, and as a consequence feasters at New Year's time have to content themselves with such viands as vegetables, fish and sweetmeats.

Well-to-do Chinamen have their reception rooms handsomely decorated at New Year's time. On the wall facing the entrance will be hung a painting representing "Good Luck," implying Sam Kup Tai—"Long life, riches and high office to you." Inscriptions in old style handwriting adorn the walls, with proverbs of the great ones of antiquity, many of them made up to suit the time and place, such as Tong wah fan hop—"Peace between China and America;" or Tong sing sai chow—"The East and West are in harmony."

CHAPTER XXIII.

CHINESE CITIZENSHIP.

CAN A CHINAMAN BECOME AN AMERICAN CITIZEN?—THE QUESTION OFTEN ASKED, BUT NOT UNDERSTOOD—NATURALIZATION OF THE MONGOLIANS.

MANY usually well informed people display a great deal of ignorance of the political status of the Mongolian residents of the United States. Are they, or can they become citizens? The doubt on this point is, perhaps, excusable because of the fourteenth amendment of the Federal Constitution adopted soon after the war period, which defines citizenship in the following manner:

"All persons born or naturalized in the United States

and subject to the jurisdiction thereof, are citizens of the United States and of the state wherein they reside."

Under this provision a Chinaman born in the United States of Chinese parents, is a citizen, and the United States Supreme Court so held in a decision recently rendered. The case that gave occasion for that decision very clearly defines the status of the Chinaman born in the United States.

Wong Kim Ark was born in San Francisco in 1873, and at the age of 17 went to China with his parents. After a brief stay he returned to the United States, and was permitted to enter on the sole ground that he was a native born citizen of the United States. In 1894 he again visited China, and returning in 1895 admission was denied him on the sole ground that he was not a citizen of the United States. He was released from custody and permitted to remain by the Federal Court, before which it was asserted and admitted that Wong Kim Ark had not, either by himself or his parents acting for him, ever renounced his allegiance to the United States, and that he had never done anything to exclude him therefrom. From this judgment the United States appealed, the result being the decision just rendered by the highest tribunal in the land, affirming the actual and complete citizenship of all persons born in this country regardless of their color or the nationality of their parents. This decision is, however, subject to the limitations of the Constitution itself, which expressly excepts "Indians not taxed." All other native born persons are citizens.

In rendering this important decision the court says:

"The opening sentence of the Fourteenth Amendment is throughout affirmative and declaratory, intended to allay doubts and settle controversies which have arisen, and not to impose any new restrictions upon citizenship. It affirms the ancient and fundamental rule of citizenship of birth within the territory, in the allegiance and under protection of this country. The amendment in clear words and by manifest intent includes the children born within the territory of the United States, of all other persons of whatever race or color domiciled within the United States. To hold that the Fourteenth Amendment excludes from citizenship the children born in the United States of citizens or subjects of other countries, would be to deny citizenship to thousands of persons of English, Scotch, Irish, German or other European parentage who have always been considered and treated as citizens of the United States."

But may a foreign born person become a citizen by the process of naturalization? That is an entirely different question. Citizenship through naturalization is confined by the terms of the Constitution to three classes of persons: 1—Free white aliens; 2—Aliens of African descent; 3—Persons of African descent, bond or free. Yet despite these limitations other classes of aliens are daily being naturalized by the courts, and thousands of Chinamen have been so naturalized. The word "white" employed in the above first class of eligibles is commonly supposed to mean Caucasian. That has been held even by the Federal Court, which ruled that "A Mongolian is not a Caucasian, and therefore not a white person." It might be added that neither is an Arab, a Hindoo, a Malay or an Egyptian. Yet persons of these nationalities are daily naturalized. Even those already citizens at times require naturalization papers for business reasons. Major General George G. Meade, who led the

Army of the Potomac during the closing year of the war, though of foreign birth, was made a citizen by virtue of a general law of Congress conferring citizenship upon all soldiers and sailors of the Union Army and Navy, was not permitted to become administrator of an estate until he produced naturalization papers, thus compelling him to go before a court, make application and go through the regular form of naturalization. It thus appears that the process of naturalization implies something more than merely making a citizen of a person. And that explains the action of the courts in naturalizing other than "white" people or those of African descent. Such naturalized persons become citizens seemingly of a restricted character. They may hold property and transact business the same as any other class of citizens, but they may not vote or hold office. "Pomeroy's Municipal Law" says: "The right of citizenship must not be confounded with the right of suffrage, and of taking part in the administration of the government." And that seems to be the status of naturalized Chinamen.

Under the decision of the Supreme Court above referred to Chinamen born in the United States, though their parents may have been subjects of the Emperor of China, are fully equipped American citizens, endowed with the same right to go and come, vote and hold office, as well as to transact business as any native born white person.

CHAPTER XXIV.

THROUGH CLOSED DOORS.

ORIGIN OF THE HOSTILITY TO CHINESE IMMIGRATION—EFFORTS OF CONGRESS TO DEBAR CHINESE LABORERS FROM THE COUNTRY—HOW THE LAW IS EVADED.

HE rapid influx of Chinese into the United States during the decade from 1875 to 1885, and the location of so many of them in California, where they threatened to monopolize various forms of unskilled labor, engendered a strong opposition to their admittance at all. This sentiment had its rise on the Pacific coast, and quickly spread among the laboring white people of that section of the country. It became so earnest that it was not placated by the efforts to retard their coming, but a labor leader of San Francisco, Dennis Kearney, launched the slogan, "The Chinese must go," which spread like wildfire. To this agitation on the western shores of the country is due, in a large measure, the restrictive legislation of Congress regarding the introduction of Chinese laborers into the United States. There has never been, nor is there now, any serious opposition to the coming and going of Chinese merchants, professional men and students, but in 1892 Congress passed an act forbidding the immigration of Chinese laborers. This law required all the Chinese then in the country to be registered by the Collector of Internal Revenue, their certificates of registration to serve as passes for them at the Custom Houses on the borders. The aim of this law was to identify the then residents and permit them, if they so desired, to revisit their native land and return here, and to keep out all newcomers of the proscribed class, who would necessarily be without certificates of registration. Strangely enough that class of the Mongolians then here and officially designated as laborers, practically refused to comply with the provisions of this law, while those of greater wealth and social distinction complied with it cheerfully. This circumstance led Congress to amend the law at its next session, by compelling all Chinamen who had not up to that time secured their registration certificates to do so within six months from the date of the passage of the act or suffer deportation. They were instructed to make application for these certificates to the officers in charge of the Internal Revenue Districts in which they resided, and furnish photographs to be attached to the certificates in duplicate. Under this law merchants and students were allowed to travel between this country and their native

China, or other countries, upon the mere prima facie proof of their standing as such. With the laborer, however, it is different. In the first place, under its provisions, if he leaves the country he is not allowed to return at all unless he can prove to the satisfaction of the Collector of Customs of the city wherein he resides that he leaves behind him a wife and children, or both, $1,000 actual debt, or that there is some blood relative dependent upon him. Even after proving either one or all three of these conditions, he must give up his registration certificate at the place of departure from the United States boundaries, taking therefor a receipt. His visit to his native land is really no more than a leave of absence for a time limit of one year from date of departure. It is only upon producing to the satisfaction of the United States representative at the city of his leave-taking the very best reasons for his remaining away longer than the original period granted, that the time will be extended, and then only upon his report being vised by the Chinese Consul, may his vacation be extended for another year. Should he fail to return to his original point of departure within the United States, and there deliver up the receipt for his registration papers, he will not be allowed to re-enter the land of the free. Should he be but one day late beyond the second year limit his certificate is confiscated and admission is refused him.

So thorough and complete are the descriptions of the registeree contained in the certificate that the authorities claim there is not one chance in a hundred of a lost or mislaid certificate being used fraudulently in smuggling another Chinaman across the border line. Each is supposed to be a record, in addition to the photographic counterfeit of the Chinaman himself, of his height, age, general characteristics of person and manner, color of hair and eyes, scars, deformities, etc., making, therefore, the smuggling of contraband Chinamen into this country, excepting as freight, or by means of impenetrable disguises, possible only with the connivance or collusion of some of the Customs service.

Still this law, rigorous and well-guarded as it seems to be, is continually evaded by the wily Chinaman. The certificates of registration are made to answer for new-comers who have been carefully coached for the ordeal they must pass through at the Custom House; or they represent themselves as merchants, students or other members of the privileged classes; sometimes they are conducted around the Custom Houses on the Canadian border, and in other ways are smuggled into this country. On the opposite page is a picture of a Chinaman now residing in Chinatown, himself a registered "laborer." His name is Jung Lee, and as a background to his picture will be seen a portion of his certificate of registration, the illustration serving to show how the photograph and certificate are put together.

JUNG LEE—A REGISTERED LABORER.

There is a moderately prosperous Chinaman now residing in Chinatown, whose principal business for several years past has been smuggling his countrymen into the United States. He has made quite a fortune for a Chinaman by his success in this questionable industry. His subjects arrive in Canada without any difficulty. They then travel to some appointed rendezvous on the northerly bank of the St. Lawrence River, where he meets them and carefully prepares them for the dash across the river, usually accompanying and guiding them. In some cases, when practicable, the newcomer is trained to take the character of a student en route for Yale or some other American college, and the necessary papers are provided for him to establish his identity, when he is enabled to advance openly and meet the Customs officials boldly. In other cases the subject is trained to represent himself as a member of some mercantile firm, the name and location of which is carefully impressed upon his mind, so that he may answer all questions without hesitation. In these and other ways thousands of these people are annually brought into the country, despite the rigors of the law forbidding them admittance.

CHAPTER XXV.

CHINESE WORSHIP.

THE RELIGIONS OF THE ORIENT—CONFUCIANISM, BUDDHISM AND TAOUISM—THE WORSHIP OF JOSS A FRAUD, NOT A FORM OF RELIGION—SOME OF ITS REPULSIVE FEATURES.

HE Chinese coming to America bring their so-called religion with them. But it is a mistake to call their superstitious idol worship and pretended forms of devotion religion. They have no religion—good, bad or indifferent. They are simply heathens—barbarians. Religion, as defined by the best lexicographers, includes the belief in the being and perfections of God or a Supreme Being, in the revelation of his will to man, in man's obligations to obey his commands, and also in the true godliness or piety of life with the practice of all moral duties. More strictly, it is said to be a belief binding the spiritual nature of man to a supernatural being on whom he is conscious that he is dependent; also the practice that springs out of the recognition of such relations, including the personal life and experience, the doctrine, the duties and rites founded on it. More generally and more comprehensively, while it means any system of faith and worship, it implies essentially a belief in a superior power or powers governing the world, and the worship of such power or powers, and the practice in life of what, by those authorities, are pronounced virtues. None of this is manifest in the so-called religion these people bring with them. The Chinese as a race are almost universally followers of Confucius, who is not even deified by them. He was simply a great philosopher, who inculcated in his writings certain principles of morality and living, mainly of a high order of merit; and while these people accept his teachings, magnifying his code of moral ethics, they do not even pretend to obey them or to practice the virtues he taught.

While claiming Confucius as their great philosopher and prophet, a large body of the Chinese at the same time claim to be Buddhists. Buddha was more of a religious teacher than was Confucius. He lived in India about 2,000 years ago, and was himself a Brahman. He taught a form of faith which might be termed a modification of Brahmanism, though based on the same view of human existence, and the same philosophy of things in general that prevail among the Brahmans.

He might have been called a reformer. He wrote nothing himself, his teachings being altogether oral. But within a hundred years after his death his disciples reduced to writing what he had taught them. From these writings the essential features of the system are gathered. It accepts, without questioning, and in its most exaggerated form, the doctrine of the transmigration of souls, which lies at the root of so much that is strange in the Eastern character.

According to Buddhist belief, when a man dies he is immediately born again, or appears in a new shape, and the same shape may, according to his merit or demerit, be any of the innumerable order of beings composing the Buddhist universe, from a clog to a divinity. If his demerit would be sufficiently punished by a degraded earthly existence—in the form, for instance, of a woman or a slave; of a persecuted or disgusting animal; of a plant, or even a piece of inorganic matter—he will be born in some one of the 136 Buddhist hells situated in the interior of the earth. These places of punishment have a regular gradation in the intensity of the suffering and in the length of time the sufferer lives, the least term of life being 10,000,000 years; the longer terms being almost beyond the power of notation to express.

A meritorious life, on the other hand, secures the next birth either in an exalted and happy position on earth, or as a blessed spirit or even divinity in one of the many heavens in which the least duration of life is about 10,000,000,000 years. But however long the life, whether of misery or bliss, it has an end, and at its close the individual must be born again, and may again be either happy or miserable, either a god or, it may be, the vilest animate object.

This system, it will be observed, recognizes a superior power, and also a future state of reward and punishment for deeds done in the body, which implies virtues to be practiced in order to gain rewards, and vices to be shunned to avoid the punishments.

Other Chinese who are not Buddhists claim to be Taouists. Laou-Tsze was a celebrated philosopher of China, the founder of a system of philosophy, accepted as a religious belief by a sect known as "Taou," or the sect of reason. Taouism dates from about 600 years before Christ. Its doctrines differ from those of Confucius and Buddha and, indeed, in their purity have a higher scope. The object of Confucius was the practical government of man through a code of morals. That of Laou-Tsze the rendering of man immortal through the contemplation of God, the repression of the passions, and the perfect tranquility of the soul. Hence his doctrine was that silence and the void produced the Taou, the "Logos" of reason by which movement was produced. And from these two sprang all beings which contained in themselves the dual principle of male and female.

Such, in brief outline, are the forms of belief supposed to be held by the Mongolians in their native land. But the ignorance of those who come to America disqualifies them from giving the distinction between the two, nor do they practice any of the virtues inculcated by either. Gambling, licentiousness, drunkenness (whether produced by the excessive use of drugs or liquors), the degradation of one's offspring—none of these practices are made virtues under any form of religious belief, but are vices, and so denounced by Confucius, Buddha and Laou-Tsze alike.

But as these vices are common among all the Chinamen who come here, full justification is afforded for the assertion that they come without any religion. Neither Confucianism, Taouism nor Buddhism (as practiced by

IN THE JOSS HOUSE.

these Orientals) maintain temples or houses of worship, nor priests, ministers, or other ecclesiastical servants. Yet they have each assumed a sort of religious character throughout the Chinese Empire, and their adherents bring such religious notions with them to this country. Yet, strange to say, as already remarked, even the most cultured and educated Chinese in America betray abject ignorance regarding these philosophies, the distinctions between them, or the difference in their inception from forms of religion.

Thus it is that the American people look upon the so-called Joss House of every Chinatown as a house of worship under one or the other of those forms of belief. It is no such thing. It is an innovation, rather—a fraud. And, by the way, it is as well to note here as elsewhere, that the name or title, "Joss," is not Chinese, but a pigeon-English word invented to signify the image worshipped, or possibly it is a corruption of the Portugese "deos"—God.

The Chinese, having forgotten the high moral principles inculcated by Confucius, and not comprehending the transcendentalism of either Buddha or Laou-Tsze, their accepted and avowed religious teachers, have set up a religion of their own, differing from either, having only ignorance and superstition for its base, and immorality for its sheet anchor. This monstrosity or travesty on religion recognizes "gods many and lords many." The image is in itself the god, not a mere representation of him. Though a divinity he is not a supreme being. It is perfectly competent and usual for any colony or company of Chinamen to set up any divinity they please, only it must be some departed being endowed with some particular claim to merit and virtue from the Chinese standpoint. Thus "Chinese Gordon," the soldier of fortune, originally of the British Army, then a leader of the government forces in China in the suppression of the Tai-ping Rebellion, and later a victim of Mahdist violence in Egypt, is now a "joss" in Chinatown.

Other josses represent departed Chinamen of alleged standing, or mythological persons of antiquity endowed with some particular virtue, or vice, for the code of these strange people recognizes but little distinction between the two elements. Monsters conspicuous in legend only for their depravity or the general viciousness of their lives, are deified as unquestionably as the purest characters in Chinese history. When a god is required to serve the purposes of any particular trade, profession or vocation, one is readily found in the musty annals of the Mongolian race, is hewed out of a block of wood, or fabricated from other materials by clever workmen, and is set up in a convenient place to receive the worship of those in need of his services.

Another point illustrating the absence of any religious element among these people is that, though they claim these images to be gods and make their prayers to and offer incense before them, they do not pray for forgiveness of sins, for help to lead better lives or for a happy future existence, but solely for material prosperity in the present life and for aid in immediately impending enterprises. The gambler prays for luck; the merchant for success in business; the highbinder for assistance in crimes; the young man for aid in securing a wife; the farmer for a good crop; the prostitute for abundant patronage; and so on through the whole range of human wants, whether good or bad. If a Chinaman wants to secure a fortune by a lottery drawing he appeals to joss to help him. Another is encumbered with female offspring, and he calls upon joss to aid in disposing of them. One has committed a serious crime, and asks for deliverance from its consequences. This one has a quarrel on his hands, and prays for aid in killing his enemy. And all these are equally devout and alike representatives of the "religion" of China.

That religion has no Sunday or holy day. With its adherents one day is as good as another, and joss is ever ready to receive the prayers and offerings of his worshippers. There is no sacredness about his dwelling place; he sits as comfortably in one place as in another, and smiles as benignantly amid clouds of opium smoke, the rivalries of a commercial rendezvous, the orgies of a vile resort where human passions have full sway, or under the gaze of a company of mere idle and curious sightseers. Nor is he at all proud and consequential. He requires no priestly intercessor between his motley worshippers and himself, nor does he call for the services of ministers or preachers to exalt his virtues and bring men to his feet. He is ever ready—for a suitable consideration—to give immediate audience to whoever wishes to approach his awful presence and proffer petitions, whether they are highborn or lowly, educated or ignorant, saints or sinners. The redhanded murderer catches his ear as readily as does the innocent victim of violence and wrong.

Joss usually sits enthroned upon a platform or dais surrounded with more or less gaudy hangings and drapings, according to the ability of those under whose patronage he may be to provide them. Essentials of his outfit are a basin filled with sand for holding the burning sticks of incense, and a prayer box. The latter is a cylindrical vessel of wood, perhaps twelve inches in height and six inches in diameter. It is filled with wooden strips slightly longer than the box itself, having an oval-shaped end. These strips are about an eighth of an inch thick, and from a half to three-quarters of an inch in width. They are all inscribed with Chinese characters which form ready-made prayers for the use of the worshippers. There is a human attendant, though having no priestly character or office. His business is to keep the place in order and to supply the customers with the essentials for their worship. These consist of half a dozen sticks of highly perfumed punk to serve as incense, two red candles, and sundry strips of paper. The whole outfit, at wholesale prices, could not cost to exceed four cents, but is sold to the worshipper for fifty cents. It must be purchased on the spot and at the established price, or that particlur joss will decline to be interviewed.

The mode of worship is interesting, but can be best comprehended by watching the movements of the worshipper. Here, for instance, comes a laundryman who has faith in lotteries and is looking for a fortune from that source. He approaches with his half dollar, which he understandingly gives to the janitor or attendant, and receives in return the requisite outfit. He then lights his red candles and sticks of incense and places them in the bowl or basin of sand in front of joss. Then he kneels and offers his prayer, which in English would be about this:

"Oh, thou great joss, thou art greater than all other gods in the universe. Your clear head and your bright genius is able to indicate the winning numbers in this slip (showing lottery ticket) which I am going to play to-night in Wing Chong Chin Company at 11 Mott Street. If you bless me with eight spots of winning on my slip I, Sing Lee, will repay your blessing with a large roasted pig, a chicken, cakes of every variety, all the fruits of the season, firecrackers by the thousands and paper money by the millions."

He then takes up the prayer box, which in this case contains 100 sticks, each stick containing one character or number, and shakes it thoroughly until one stick falls out. Whatever number happens to be on this stick he accepts as joss' indications of the winning number he is to play, and hurries away to the lottery shop to invest his money on that number—and lose it.

Now you observe the devotions of Mr. Lee Wah Sing, an earnest young man who is anxious to purchase a certain young girl for a concubine. He approaches joss in the same manner as did Sing Lee, having obtained from the attendant a similar outfit. In addition he must have in writing the name of the girl who is for sale, her age, birthday, the town of her nativity, and the necessary data for her identification. He then lights incense sticks, kneels and makes his prayer, beginning with a like fulsome laudation of Joss' powers, asking his aid in securing the girl he wants, and promises similar generous returns as did Sing Lee. He then takes the prayer box, the numbers in which in this case correspond to certain numbers and verses in a prayer book which the attendant hands him free of other charge after having paid fifty cents for his incense. If he finds the indicated verse in the prayer book is favorable to his amorous wish he takes his girl and pays for her. But if the answer is unfavorable he drops her and goes in pursuit of another.

Here comes a man who wants to consult Joss in regard

'SHALL I BUY THE LAUNDRY?'

to the purchase of a certain laundry. He goes through the same preliminaries as the others, but does not make use of the prayer box. Instead he is supplied with two kidney-shaped pieces of wood. One side of each of these pieces is designated head and the other tail. After he has called upon Joss in the general terms of his predecessors, he tosses the two pieces of wood up. If they fall with two heads it means pretty good; if one head and one tail, very good; if two tails, the meaning is very bad. His negotiations for the laundry will be governed by these indications of the estimate Joss puts upon the business.

All Chinatown was greatly excited during the early part of the present year because of the prevalence of sickness among its denizens. Immediately after the Chinese New Year, January 27, there were more than twenty deaths. Nearly every day Chinamen of more or less distinction died.

At the beginning of the new year the Mayor of Chinatown, according to custom, makes an official devotion to the Joss enthroned at headquarters. He did so this year, and on taking the praying machine shook out stick No. 10, which indicated this prophecy in the book of prophecies, meaning, according to Chinese lore, that sickness and death would prevail throughout the year in Chinatown. The translated prophecy reads:

"At time of sickness life lingers around;
Why break the roof or chain the turtle?
Strict obedience is sure to reign,
But trust in Joss and Buddha is the only remedy."

This is much more like a religious act than the illustrations that precede it. But all alike show the basis of superstition and ignorance upon which the structure stands. Its absolute distinction from Buddhism or Taouism is manifest. It has nothing in common with either, though is doubtless an outgrowth of both systems, tinctured somewhat with Confucianism, the foundation of which is filial respect and duty, which might well lead to ancestral worship. But as practiced, the so-called religion calls for no worship, and none such is performed. What passes for worship is a mere superstitious invocation of assistance in impending need or distress. Nothing beyond the immediate temporal or sensual requirements of the devotee is even thought of. There is no adoration of the pretended divinity; no manifestation of repentance for sins or a desire for a holier life; no recognition of a future state of rewards or punishments. The same god is recognized and appealed to by the vilest or the most virtuous person.

Nor is there any general assemblage for worship and praise, as provided in both the Christian and Jewish systems of religion; merely the individual appeals as already shown. There are no Sabbaths or other holy days. There is no religion about it except the selfish and greedy needs of the moment. All the ancient Oriental systems of religion recognize and inculcate substantially the same code of morals as does the Christian church of to-day. The entire philosophy of Confucius is based on the fifth commandment of the Decalogue and the Golden Rule—honor to parents, and doing to others as we would have others do to us.

Buddha taught right living in this life as essential to a happy future. Laou-Tsze dwelt on the contemplation of heavenly things as an incentive to holy living in preparation for an exalted state of future existence. None of these features are to be found in the joss worship of to-day. That worship calls for no higher religious incentive than moves one to consult a fortune teller.

Despite all this, however, there is some religious spirit among these people. There is a disciple of Confucius among them who assembles as many of the faithful as he can gather on Sunday afternoons in the halls of the Chong Wah Gong Shaw and discourses to them on the teachings of their master; exhorting them to perseverance in the faith. This man's name is Chi Kai Pik, one of the secretaries of the Chinese Consulate. His topics sound very queer to outsiders. Thus he has given a series of three discourses, the topics of which were: 1—"Kut Pot ching, pot shak" (Not cut squarely, I shall not eat). 2—"Pot she, pot shak, pot" (Not in season I shall not eat). 3—"Tuck ke tsou, pot shak" (Without sauce I shall not eat). The word used to mean "squarely" implics honesty. "Season" implies time and circumstances, a clear conscience. "Tsou" means, literally, "sauce;" but as used here implies grace. Thus it can be readily seen that under these hyperbolic titles a vast deal of substantial truth and sound moral principle can be conveyed. And that is far more profitable and elevating than prostrating oneself before a wooden image or a hideous daub and appealing to it for help in gambling or guidance in the purchase of human flesh for beastly uses. The two are radically antagonistic. The one possesses a smattering of religion—moral improvement; the other is debasing, demoralizing and utterly devoid of any religious flavor. The expenses of this weekly Confucian service are defrayed by the Chinese Government through its minister at Washington

CHAPTER XXVI.

RESTLESS BONES.

AN ILLUSTRATION OF CHINESE SUPERSTITION—WHY THE REMAINS OF DEAD CHINAMEN MUST BE RETURNED TO THE CELESTIAL EMPIRE—HOW THE WORK OF THEIR RECOVERY AND SHIPMENT IS PERFORMED.

HE intense superstition of the Chinese is displayed in nothing more clearly than in the matter of the disposal of their remains after death. It was a matter of universal comment when the great Li Hung Chang, the most intelligent Chinaman of the age, made his famous tour of Europe and America, that he carried a coffin with him, and his servants were instructed, in case of his death, to place his body in the coffin and take it back to China for burial. On this point his orders were most emphatic and rigid. So also the humblest Chinaman cannot be induced to leave his native land until assured that, should he die while abroad, his remains will be returned for final interment in the sacred soil of the Celestial Empire. Their anxiety in this respect has much to do with the company craze which possesses them. The famous Six Companies which now figure so prominently in all that relates to the Chinese residing in this country, were originally formed chiefly to attend to the return of the remains of dead Chinamen to China. When other matters began to engross the attention of those companies to such an extent that they grew careless in the discharge of their original duty, the immigrants began to form other societies composed of those coming from any particular district, with no other purpose than the rescue and return home of the bones of their members. Then as trade organizations began to multiply among them their leaders charged themselves, as a part of their vocation, with the pious duty of guarding the remains of their members who might die, and seeing that they were returned to the sacred soil.

But despite all these agencies, American soil is still the resting place of many of these Mongolian bodies. This is due to the great numbers of them who come here; to their wide dispersion over the country from the Atlantic to the Pacific; to the nomadic habits of many of them; to the isolated places in which they many times find themselves; but more especially to the disinclination of the authorities in many cases, for sanitary reasons, to allow disinterments. This latter reason was originally conceived in San Francisco by the radical anti-Chinese people, and was pressed purely to vex and annoy the Chinese, and so discourage their coming to the United States.

A CHINESE FUNERAL.

But there is no doubt good foundation for objecting to such disinterment by wholesale, and the Boards of Health of this and other large communities have felt compelled to adopt strict regulations regarding it as a precaution against endangering the public health.

The insistence of the Chinese on having their remains returned to China for final burial is based wholly upon the superstition that otherwise their spirits will be troubled and without rest or peace in their future state of existence. They will also be exposed to the assaults and persecutions of every form of malevolent devils; will be beaten, tortured and driven about, and will, in fact, be compelled to exist in a veritable hell until their bones find shelter beneath the sacred soil of the Celestial land, when their troubles will end and their spirits will be at rest.

Chinamen have been coming to this city for fully half a century, but not in any great numbers until within the last fifteen or twenty years. The earlier immigrants were notably of a higher grade, intellectually and physically, at least, than those who have more recently poured in upon us. But these earlier comers, being stragglers, had nobody to look after their remains if they died while here. And so it happens that occasional burials of these people have been made in these years. Many of the early comers were undoubtedly buried in the paupers' burying ground, and their graves are now indistinguishable. But since there has been a regular colony of them here more care has been taken in the disposal of the remains of their dead, with a view to their subsequent recovery and shipment to their native land. With this end in view ground was purchased in the New York Bay Cemetery, in the Greenville section of Jersey City, where they were interred. For economy's sake bodies were buried as many as possible in a single grave, the coffins resting one on top of the other, until so near the surface that no more would be permitted by the cemetery authorities. This arrangement sadly mixed the bodies, so that now it is found difficult to separate and identify them. At least fifty have been buried in those grounds; others found sepulchre in Greenwood, while still others lie scattered in various cemeteries throughout all this region.

Later a plot was secured in the Cemetery of the Evergreens, Brooklyn, which is commonly known as Celestial Hill, and here the Chinamen who have died of late years have been interred. Hundreds of burials have taken place there, and they are still being added to continually. It is now the only recognized Chinese burial ground in this vicinity.

The exhumation of the remains of the neglected ones was made a philanthropic duty by Ching Wah and Kung Saw a few years ago, acting under the auspices of the Chinese legation. They employed two Chinese laborers to assist them, though the graves were opened by the regular grave diggers of the cemetery These, however, are only permitted to uncover the coffins, the actual remains being considered too sacred to be even touched by other hands than those of their countrymen. When recovered the remains are taken to a tent near at hand where a charcoal furnace is provided, over which the portions of the body, after being carefully segregated, are dried and the remaining flesh burned off. The bones are then scraped and thoroughly cleaned, after which they are wrapped in excelsior and packed in boxes, each box containing only the bones of one individual, and marked with the name and date of death of the person in Chinese characters, for identification in China. The boxes are then ready for shipment.

The expenses of the general recovery and return of these bodies are defrayed by subscription among the Chinese themselves, though if any of the deceased left estates, or have relatives who can bear the expense, these sources are looked to in the individual cases, only the bones of the poor and friendless being recovered at the expense of the common fund. There is a legend afloat in Chinatown that the spirit of a deceased Chinaman who was buried in Greenwood Cemetery appeared to the Mayor of Chinatown and complained that he, and others buried with him, could get no rest because of the "white devils" among whom they were lying. This apparition, so the story goes, was followed by others, until the matter was referred to a committee of the Chong Wah Gong Shaw, who decided to purchase the plot in the Cemetery of Evergreens, where all the Chinamen who have since died have been buried.

The recovery of the bones of buried Chinamen in this country and their return to China is by no means the only occasion on which these curious people meddle with the remains of their dead. In Formosa the dead bodies are exposed and dried in the open air, and when the flesh has withered away, the bones are cleansed and preserved. In other portions of the empire the bodies are buried, it is true, but after a year or more, having selected a lucky day, the relatives disinter them, take out the bones, brush and wash them clean, then wrap them in cloth and return them to the grave.

In this connection a queer and superstitious custom of these people regarding their dead may properly be

A SCENE IN EVERGREEN CEMETERY.

briefly noticed. Ts'ing Ming is the period in the Chinese calendar corresponding with the early part of our month of April. At this time is performed the rite of worship at the ancestral tombs. This is regarded as a most sacred duty by all Chinamen, and he who would wilfully fail in performing it would be looked upon as an outcast. Hence its observance by the Chinamen of New York.

As but few of these have ancestors buried in this country, while those who are buried here have only occasionally relatives in this country to pay their remains this reverence, it has become the custom for "cousins" and friends to perform the ceremony. On the morning of the day in question the male members of the family in China, or the friends and relatives of the deceased in this country, repair to the place of burial, where, having weeded and swept the grave, they light incense and arrange beside or upon it sacrificial offerings of roast pigs and fowls, fish, cakes, tea, wine, cigarettes and whatever else may minister to the comfort of the departed one. The family representative (or here the nearest relative) then performs the Ko-t'ow in honor of the deceased, and each in turn follows his example. Papers representing money are then burned, on the ashes of which are poured libations of wine. A second Ko-t'ow ends the ceremony.

This ceremony can be observed in Evergreen Cemetery at Celestial Hill, on the first Sunday of April in every year and on the Monday following. It calls Chinamen by the hundreds to the burying ground. The prosperous merchant and his friends come in carriages, their offerings being brought in express wagons; the laundrymen ride to the cemetery gates in the surface or elevated street cars, and then proceed on foot, carrying their offerings in baskets and huge bundles.

They chatter and laugh and smoke on the way as if never troubled with sorrow, and perform the ceremony at the grave in the same hilarious, unconcerned manner. When through they wait for the spirit of the departed to make a hurried meal of the essential and immaterial elements of the viands offered, and then, gathering up the substantial food, return to town and enjoy the feast it affords. Whole roasted pigs by the score appear among these offerings; chickens and ducks by the hundreds; besides boiled rice and various kinds of cakes and sweetmeats.

CHAPTER XXVII.

MISSIONARY WORK AMONG THE CHINESE.

EFFORTS MADE TO CONVERT THE HEATHEN TO CHRISTIANITY—VARIOUS MISSIONS ESTABLISHED AMONG THEM—WHAT IS BEING ACCOMPLISHED IN THIS DIRECTION.

HINATOWN, in the center of New York, furnishes opportunity for observing the antithesis of heathenism and Christianity; the contrast of the most ancient with the most advanced forms of civilization; the advantages of liberty of thought, of action and of person over the blighting conservatism of the Orient, which forbids progress in any form, and binds its subjects to the habits, customs and manners of the musty past.

Here in Chinatown is seen the struggle for supremacy of superstition over intelligence and reason, a strange intermingling of vice and crime upon a common plane with morality and virtue; the worship of images rather than the one only living and true God; wickedness of the most repulsive character recognized as equally meritorious with honest business industry; honor and shame standing side by side, and both alike commanding recognition and respect; ignorance and squalor, human slavery, women treated as chattels, gambling made a pursuit as reputable and deserving as any respectable productive industry; the vile opium smoking dens as well as the headquarters of the organization of cutthroats, thieves and robbers, made places wherein "the gods made by men's hands" are worshipped, and whose power is invoked for aid in the prosecution of crimes and business projects alike.

In the language of another, "the philosophical doctrines of Laou-Tsze, of the identity of existence and non-existence, imbibed by these ignorant people, become to them a warrant for the old epicurean motto, 'Let us eat and drink, for to-morrow we die.' The pleasures of sense were substituted by them for the delights of virtue, and finally all became a sort of religion claiming the homage of the race." And this so-called religion is now installed in Chinatown under the very shadow of Christian temples and within hearing of the voices of those who teach and preach the religion of Jesus Christ.

The earnest Christian is commanded by his Master: "Go and preach the Gospel to all men," and millions of dollars are annually contributed to maintain Christian missions in heathen lands. But here is a heathen colony planted in the very midst of a Christian city which is looked to as the chief reliance for the support of foreign missions. If the Christian religion is the only true form of faith and doctrine—which we are not permitted to doubt —and if Christian civilization is so vastly superior, how does it happen that this paganism can be maintained right here in the midst of Christian churches and peoples, where the Christian bible is freely circulated and may be read by all men, and enveloped, so to speak, by Christian civilization of the most advanced type? The two stand in close juxtaposition. If the doctrine of the survival of the fittest has any real foundation, one or the other of these religions and civilizations must give way to the other.

The Christian churches and people of New York have not been and are not now neglectful of their duty regarding this intrusion of heathenism among them, although possibly all has not been done that might and should be done for the conversion of these benighted people, or for their moral enlightenment. There are scores of Christian missionaries working in Chinatown, and a number of regular missions maintained there. And throughout the city the various churches seem disposed to gather in the scattered heathens employed in their parishes as laundrymen, servants or laborers, and teach them, in Sunday Schools, the rudiments of Christianity. Of the work in Chinatown more will be said further on. Of the work in Sunday Schools in various parts of the city what there is to be said might as well be said right here and now. There are no available statistics of the number of these Sunday School classes maintained; of the aggregate attendance in them; nor of the results accomplished. But there is good ground for questioning their efficiency as religious agencies. That they attract attendants is manifest. But a little investigation will disclose the fact that the pupils so attracted are chiefly those who are more desirous of learning the English language than the Christian religion. The classes are mostly taught by young white women, themselves absolutely ignorant regarding the Chinese language. They may be ever so earnest and zealous, but manifestly they can impart no religious instruction until they have first taught their pupils to read, or at least speak and understand English; and when the pupils have attained that much, they, as a majority, have obtained all they want. They do not care to remain longer to learn of a religion they have only heard of as antagonistic to that of their ancestors, whom they have been taught to venerate and worship. Some few of them, in too many cases attracted by the pretty faces of their teachers, do remain longer, and quite too often have succeeded in capturing their teachers' hearts and making wives of them. True, in most cases, conversion must at least be pretended before the capture can be effected.

Because of this result a number of churches that formerly maintained such classes have been led to abandon them, and others are considering the problem whether the good accomplished justifies the exposure of their young and sentimental female members to this temptation. For with all the boasted charity they profess—that charity which is counted the greatest of all virtues—these Christian churches are not yet ready to admit the equality of the races, nor to sanction the inter-marriage of their young female members with these, to them, uncouth and heathen, if not actually repulsive, Orientals, even though the latter be alleged to be "Christianized."

The regular missions now maintained in Chinatown, and employing missionaries who work as well among the scattered Chinamen through the city, are, however, performing legitimate missionary work in a perfectly legitimate manner. Most of these employ converted Chinamen, who have been educated for the ministry as missionaries, and these are able to do effective work in preaching the gospel to their countrymen, and in laboring with them individually.

METHODIST MISSIONS.

The Chinese Mission of the Methodist Episcopal Church, now established in the building of the Methodist Book Concern at 150 Fifth Avenue, is really the pioneer of Christian effort among the Chinese of this city. It was originally established in 1878, at 14 Mott Street, by Mr. Moy Jin Kee, a converted Chinaman, who had become a member of the Methodist Episcopal Church within the province of the New York East Conference. The teachers of the mission came from the churches of that denomination in New York and Brooklyn, and the superintendent was the late Rev. Dr. C. S. Brown, then of the Five Points Mission. The average evening attendance at the week night school of this mission was about eighteen, and the Sunday attendance reached as high as eighty.

Among the teachers at this mission were Jacob H. V. Cockcroft, Mrs. Henrietta Millwood, now a police matron in Brooklyn; Miss Mary Alice, a daughter of Rev. Dr. Brown; Mrs. Joseph Skidmore, now deceased; Mr. Edward E. Pidgeon, now a prominent New York newspaper man, and Mr. William S. Baxter, at present engaged in missionary work in China.

When Moy Jin Kee was called to other work, Rev. James Jackson, now a missionary at Wu Chang, China,

MOY JIN KEE.

succeeded him in charge of the mission. At the end of a year the mission was removed to the Seventh Street M. E. Church, and on the Rev. Mr. Jackson's return to China, Dr. Jin Fuey Moy, a brother of Moy Jin Kee, succeeded as superintendent. Later on the mission was removed to the southwest corner of Seventh Avenue and Twenty-third Street, and finally to its present location in the building of the Methodist Book Concern, No. 150 Fifth Avenue.

Referring to the work of converting the Chinese to Christianity, Dr. Jin. Fuey Moy said to the writer:

"I don't think the missionaries will ever succeed in Christianizing the Chinese of this city until they first root out the evils of Chinatown—the contaminating influences of gambling and prostitution. As things are now, the Chinese go from the houses of prostitution and gambling to the Sunday Schools, and from the Sunday Schools to the houses of gambling and prostitution. As a rule this is one great drawback. The Chinese do not care anything about the Christian religion, but only go to the missions and Sunday Schools for the purpose of learning the English language. They realize that to carry on business with any success among the English speaking people they must learn the English language. Here is their great opportunity—and it costs them nothing—and many of them go no further in that direction than the fifth reader. When they get to the point where they have mastered the fifth reader they consider that they have acquired a sufficient vocabulary to enable them to carry on successfully the intercourse of their different vocations and therefore cease to attend the missions and

Sunday Schools longer. Naturally there are exceptions, however, and many brilliant ones right in New York."

REV. SOULE BOK'S REPORT.

Rev. C. Soule Bok, a native Chinaman, who is working as a missionary among his countrymen in this city, under the auspices of this Methodist Episcopal Church Mission, contributes to The Christian City, the local missionary organ of that denomination, the following interesting report of his evangelistic labors:

"During the last ten or fifteen years thousands of Chinese have migrated toward the East, until now the Chinese population numbers about ten thousand souls in Greater New York.

"The missionary spirit that moved God's people in California has also moved the people here, of various denominations, to open their church doors for the Chinese, wherein they may learn the way of life.

"Our Methodist school was started in 1884, in the Eighteenth Street Methodist Episcopal Church, by a young Christian Chinese, one of the government students. When Miss Mary A. Lathbury and Mrs. S. J. Brigham, her sister, returned from their summer vacation that year they became identified with this school. Miss Lathbury was made superintendent after Messrs. Woo, Lee, and Kwai, all of whom were government students. Mrs. Brigham assisted the superintendent and was the teacher of a class of which the present writer, he is proud to say, was a member.

"This same school became a mission in 1888, when we moved from the church to a house, corner of Twenty-third Street and Seventh Avenue. We now meet in the Methodist Book Concern Building, 150 Fifth Avenue,

New York, within the very walls whence missionaries are sent out by this church.

"Our Sunday School meets every Sunday afternoon at 2.30 o'clock. Pupils are taught in groups of two, three, four or six, around small tables. They begin with A, B, C, and degree by degree advance up to the Bible itself. After they have studied an hour or so with their teachers, the superintendent then translates the lesson before them all with opened book into their own tongue, after which he makes brief remarks upon the lesson.

"The Young Men's Prayer Meeting, or Y. M. C. A., held after the school, at 4.15, is a strong support to the mission. The meetings are conducted entirely in the Chinese language, both in singing and in speaking, and are led by one of the members appointed by the President, who is a student in New York University, from week to week, until all have led.

"Through this mission thirty-two souls have been gathered together into Christ's kingdom since 1884; about twenty-five hundred names have been enrolled in our book, of men who have come to us for instruction for longer or shorter periods.

"Some of the thirty-two Christians who have returned to their mother country felt the need of a place of worship. Accordingly they have raised among themselves three hundred dollars for the building of a church, and have sent us word for aid. Pray that their need may soon be met. We have a Missionary Society in our mission founded only recently, and a collection is taken each month for the above church building fund.

"There are twenty-two Sunday Schools and Missions in New York and Brooklyn for the Chinese. Only thirteen hundred of the entire population of 10,000 are reached with Christian instruction. Eighty-seven hundred are not reached! Unless efforts shall soon be made to save these human souls they will die without hearing of Christ. The question that is confronting us to-day is, how, since most of these people have not sufficient knowledge of English to hear the Gospel in American churches, can they hear it at all, unless it is brought to them in their own tongue?

"A little more than two years ago three young men, two of the Congregational Church, the third a Methodist, who felt most keenly concerning the lost condition of these 8,700 souls, came together and gave the matter to prayer. A week after this meeting invitations were sent out to all Christians of all schools of various denominations to meet with the three. The formation of a society was the result, the name of which is called The Chinese Evangelical Band. In this same meeting twenty men pledged themselves to give a dollar a month for the support of the work. Two weeks after a parlor floor was secured at No. 8 Pell Street, New York, in a neighborhood where about three thousand Chinese reside during the week and on Sunday from seven to ten thousand come from all parts of Greater New York.

"Our immediate need now is more suitable and larger quarters. We have now five hundred dollars put away as a building fund. This would perhaps be enough to buy a few bricks; yet a single drop of water will not form an ocean, nor will a few bricks build a house. We must, therefore, first do all we can and look to God for the rest."

BAPTIST MISSIONS.

The only fully organized mission now maintained in Chinatown proper is the Morning Star Mission, at 17

Doyers Street, which is conducted under the auspices of the American Baptist Home Mission Society. This mission was established about six years ago by Miss Helen Clark. It occupies the entire second floor of the building, having well lighted apartments with windows on three sides. During the week a night school is conducted here for education in English for young and old, white and Mongol, which is opened and closed with religious exercises. It has about twenty-three attendants on the average. Two afternoons each week a white physician is in attendance to advise and prescribe for all comers free of charge. Medicines are also dispensed.

During the first year of this particular work over five hundred Chinese were prescribed for. On Sunday afternoons and evenings religious exercises are conducted here. The first is a meeting of the Young Men's Christian Association, composed exclusively of Chinese young men. The services consist mainly of the singing of gospel hymns and relation of Christian experience by the converted members. This is followed by Sunday School, conducted in English, at which the teachers are male and female volunteers from the city churches. There are twenty or more of these volunteer teachers, and an average attendance of eighty-three Chinese pupils. At 8 o'clock a regular service is held in the Chinese language by the Rev. Fung Y. Mow, the missionary representing the Home Mission Society. He preaches to his countrymen in their own tongue, and is well received. A prayer meeting closes the day's exercises, which have been continuous for six or eight hours. Joe Gum, a converted Chinaman, assists the missionary, and Tong Gow serves as organist.

This mission is superintended by the Fifth Avenue

Baptist Church, of which Rev. Dr. Faunce is pastor. It is under the immediate charge of an advisory board of seven members of the church. Among those interested in the work, and one of the most liberal contributors to its support, is Mr. John D. Rockefeller, of Standard Oil fame.

Rev. Fung Yet Mow, the missionary, was born in Canton, China, thirty-two years ago. He came to this country in 1882, and studied at the Baptist Mission School in San Francisco, from which he graduated. He returned to China on a visit, but was asked by the Baptist Home Mission Society to return to this country and serve as a missionary, which he did. While in China he was married to a young Chinese woman, a daughter of a deacon of the First Baptist Church in Canton, who was a graduate of the American Medical College of Canton, where she took the degree of M. D.

Mr. Mow returned to this country seven years ago, accompanied by his wife, and commenced his missionary labors in San Francisco under Dr. J. B. Hartwell, superintendent on the Pacific coast of the Baptist Home Mission Society. He came to New York five years ago and continued his work as a missionary in the Morning Star Mission.

Mr. Mow, who lives in Brooklyn, is soon to be ordained a minister of the Baptist Church. He has now been a missionary for about twelve years and has accomplished much good among his fellow countrymen. His father-in-law has been a Christianized Chinaman for upwards of forty years, in his own land, where, in consequence, he has been subjected to many persecutions by his ignorant countrymen. Rev. Tee Tsai Leung, of Chicago, a Baptist minister in charge of the work of the Home Mission Society in that city, is a brother-in-law of Mr. Mow. Although Mr. Mow's wife is a regular graduated doctor of the American Medical School in Canton, and obtained her degree of M. D., she does not practice her profession.

Rev. Fung Yet Mow, when asked if he thought Chinatown was a better place to-day than it was ten years ago, said:

"Yes, I think that Chinatown is a great deal better to-day than it was ten years ago. Ten years ago respectable people were afraid to pass through Pell and Doyers Streets after dark for fear of being assaulted by the toughs, both Chinamen and whites, who infested the neighborhood. Since the mission was started all this has been changed, and Chinatown is a better place to-day than it was before I came here."

Mr. Mow states that many young men, students from Simpson's College, Forty-eighth Street and Eighth Avenue, come down to Chinatown on Sunday to teach in the mission and distribute tracts in the homes of the Chinese, and in this way the Gospel is carried into many dwellings, great good resulting. Many converted Chinamen return to China to labor as missionaries among the people of their native land. He has sent four converts home since he has had charge of the work.

Most of the Chinamen in the colony receive Mr. Mow cordially when he calls on them, and do not seem to think he is antagonistic to their religion. Mr. Mow says that thirty-five or forty Chinamen of all classes have been converted under his ministrations. He visits the sick Chinamen when they are taken to the hospitals, and when they are sick at their homes he secures medical attendance for them.

In connection with the work of the Morning Star Mission much is being done for the children of Chinatown. On the second floor of 21 Mott Street, Miss Helen Clark is in charge of the Evangelical Mission. There is a day school of twenty-five pupils in the mission. On Sundays the teachers make the rounds of the tenements of the Chinese quarter seeking juvenile attendants, as the parents, who may still cling to their heathen notions, would never send their youngsters voluntarily. At first, as a rule, they resent all such overtures, but when they see how much trouble the teachers take with the children they allow them to visit the mission, provided the little ones are anxious. On an average they secure about thirty children each Sunday. This is much better than a few years ago, when the parents made every excuse for keeping their little ones at home. The teachers use pictures in illustrating the lessons and the children seem to take an interest in what is told them. The teachers find that in a short time some of the pupils know considerable of the Gospel, and carry what they learn to their parents.

The knowledge of the New Light is received with anything but joy in the heathen household, as may be gleaned from the words of one of the teachers, who said:

"I wish I could tell you how many of the children are Christians, but we are praying for more. It is very hard for a Chinese child to be a Christian. Not long ago a Chinese father told his boy, who had been attending our school, to place incense before the idol on one of the altars in his home. The boy did not want to do so and took the incense reluctantly, slowly walked toward the altar, and just as slowly reached up toward it. The father, understanding his son's motives for his conduct, snatched up a stick and struck him such a blow on the head that the boy fell back almost senseless.

"They tell us that they want to love Jesus, but few of them dare say so at home."

While Miss Clark is teaching in the school other teachers visit the homes and try to show the Chinese women the Christian way of living. Almost all are quite willing to listen and want to know about the "Jesus doctrine," and would become Christians were they free to act for themselves. But they think they are under their father, husband or other relative, and must cling to their idolatry when their relatives so command. Recently one of the women said:

"I want to love Jesus, but my husband won't let me. But maybe by and by he and all of us will be Christians."

EVANGELICAL BAND.

In the year 1895 about twenty-four Chinese young men, interested in the welfare of their countrymen, devised a plan to convert them. They accordingly organized the Evangelical Band, and each member was assessed $1 a month as dues in order to sustain the band. Three or four months after their organization they founded a mission at No. 8 Pell Street and engaged one room, about fourteen feet square, for the purpose of inducing Chinamen to come to the meetings where the Gospel of Christ was preached. The attendance was generally more than could be accommodated, and they have had as many as 115 attendants at their Sunday night services. When this was noticed by the other churches interested in the Chinese the band was invited to give a brief history of its work, and from each church where the work was made known they have since received contributions in order to enable them to continue it. There is now a membership of 224 Chinamen in the band, each of whom contributes $1 towards its support each month. Chin K. Kiu is the president of the band.

Another mission maintained in Chinatown is a union, or non-sectarian enterprise, under the direction of Mrs. Blanchard, of 2,100 Madison Avenue. It leases a hall at No. 8 Pell Street, employing for that purpose such students or ministers capable of expounding the Gospel in the Chinese language as it can secure from time to time. It also holds prayer and song services, besides visiting among the Chinese.

The Rescue Mission is also doing considerable work in Chinatown, though chiefly in the line of its own specialty, the recovery and reformation of fallen women. There is quite a plenty of this work to be done in that locality, but as the depraved women of that neighborhood, as well as elsewhere in the city, are mainly whites, the work of the Rescue Mission has no special bearing upon the Chinese.

Mrs. Josephine Williamson, who has long been identified with the work of seeking to rescue fallen women here, might contribute many an interesting page of the history of Chinatown by night, of which the following is but a fair sample:

"A dozen women were found," she says, "several of whom had been legally married by the Methodist and other Christian rites, to their pig-tailed companions, and were cleanly and happy. They all knew some of the visitors, and knelt dutifully when prayer was offered. The Chinamen, accustomed to this sort of intrusion on their domesticity, paid no heed whatever to it. In one little room where a docile and pretty girl of the name of Jennie claimed a Chinaman as her legal husband, the spouse and two friends were playing cards. They kept right on with the game through prayer and all, just as if no one had come in."

Mrs. Williamson also tells of her experience in the opium dens of Chinatown. "I have seen white girls in the dens of Chinatown completely enthralled by it (opium smoking). The deadly drug makes her as unconscious of her companion's brutality as it does of her own degradation."

Halting at the door of one of these places on one occasion Mrs. Williamson peered in. "On bunks," she said, "stretched out in various graceless attitudes, in a state of semi-stupor, were probably thirty Chinamen and a few girls, who partly unclosed their heavy eyes to leer at the intruders. The praying band did not remain here long, but went up another flight of stairs, where, in the hall, leaning against the staircase were a dozen Chinamen and as many girls smoking cigarettes."

The praying band entered the room of one of the girls known as Kitty. "Oh, what a poor, wretched little room. The walls of pine board were paperless. On the floor a few strips of faded carpet were laid. In one corner was a neatly made bed. A cooking stove, a table on which stood a lamp and a few pictures completed the furniture. There was a pitiful attempt at decoration, however, which indicated that desire latent in every woman to beautify the place in which she lives. The window over the door was draped with what was certainly a dress flouncing of lace, while at each corner were knots of faded blue ribbon. A photograph of a Chinaman had a twist of dirty pink silk around it, probably the remains of a ball dress. There were a few pictures on the wall suggestive of a life of virtuous domesticity. There was one, a grandmother in a cap, knitting, while two children watched a kitten play with the ball of yarn. Another represented a girl in bridal array, while her prospective husband waits her coming at the door with a look of exultant happiness on his face, as portrayed by a highly tinted chromo. Still another is called the "First Born." The same couple are leaning over a crib regarding a sleeping infant with expressions of rapture."

These brief sketches will serve to illustrate the depravity of Chinatown, as well as the manner in which Christian effort for its reformation is exerted.

It would be interesting to give, in this connection, some estimate of the progress that is being made in the work of civilizing and Christianizing these heathens. On that point, however, there is no reliable data at hand. Each church and each missionary organization reports, in a general way, much success in its work, and all claim converts to Christianity. Undoubtedly many such converts have been made, some of whom are now at work, as has been seen, endeavoring to win other of their countrymen to the Religion of the Cross. Others are being educated under the influence of the white Christian ministers, and are now employed in the various foreign missionary societies and boards, as missionaries in China. But it is a mistaken notion that every Chinaman who has cast aside his queue and native dress for that of Western civilization has become a Christian. He may have become Christianized, which is a term used to designate those who have rejected the errors and superstitions of the Orient, with its false idea of religion, though without conversion to the faith of the Gospel. The term Americanized would more correctly indicate this class. They have undoubtedly been brought to their present half-way state through missionary efforts; but they are very far from being Christians. And possibly there are more of this class than the really converted. They have been brought to see the superiority of Christian civilization, and to adopt it, outwardly at least. But they have not discarded the vices which are common alike to Orientals and Occidentals. They are simply in the same frame of mind as the Roman ruler who, after listening to the eloquent reasoning of the Apostle Paul, exclaimed: "Almost thou persuadest me to be a Christian." But that ruler was not altogether persuaded, nor are these "Christianized" Chinamen. The work of evangelizing them is yet to be accomplished, and it is a much more difficult task than merely relieving them of the outward garb of heathenism.

Mr. Charles D. Kellogg, Secretary of the Charities Organization Society, Fourth Avenue and Twenty-third Street, furnished the following list of Chinese missions maintained in this city and Brooklyn. Though registered as missions the most of these are but Sunday Schools, though conducted on more substantial lines than the ordinary church Sunday Schools above referred to. Some of them have Christian Chinamen attached as missionaries and teachers. The list is as follows:

Chinese Mission of the Pilgrim Congregational Church, Madison Avenue and 121st Street. Rev. Dr. Virgin, pastor and manager.

City Mission and Tract Society, United Charity Building, Fourth Avenue and 121st Street.

Chinese Mission of the Methodist Episcopal Church, 150 Fifth Avenue. See Soule Bok, Superintendent.

Presbyterian Chinese Mission and School, 53 Fifth Avenue. Huie Kin, Manager.

Chinese Mission, South Oxford Street, Brooklyn. Mrs. N. B. Sizer, Manager, 336 Greene Avenue, Brooklyn.

Chinese Mission of the Central Congregational Church, Brooklyn. Miss Z. Dowie, 164 Gates Avenue, Brooklyn.

Phoenix Hall Chinese Mission, 118 South Eighth Street, Brooklyn. Miss Annie Hollu.

South Brooklyn Chinese Mission, Fourth Avenue and Fifteenth Street, Brooklyn. Michael Hamilton, Superintendent.

De Witt Memorial of the New York Tract Society, 280 Rivington Street. Rev. William T. Ellsing, Superintendent.

Chinese Mission of St. Andrew's P. E. Church, Fifth Avenue and 127th Street. Rev. George Van de Water, Rector.

Chinese Mission of St. Thomas' P. E. Church, Fifth Avenue and 53d Street. Rev. J. Wesley Brown, Rector; James Pott, Superintendent.

CHAPTER XXVIII.

GEORGE APPO—BORN TO CRIME.

THE SON OF A MURDERER, AFTER SPENDING HALF HIS LIFE IN PRISON, FOLLOWS IN THE FOOTSTEPS OF HIS FATHER TO A CELL FOR THE INSANE.

EORGE APPO was born in New York City, July 4, 1858, and is therefore an American citizen, and should be a patriotic one, but he is not. His father was a full-blooded Chinaman and his mother an Irish woman. He was an exceedingly bright child, beautiful to look upon, sharp-witted and quick of comprehension. For ten years he was the pet of the neighborhood where his parents dwelt, and during that time had abundant opportunity to acquaint himself with many forms

GEORGE APPO.

of vice. After a careful consideration he selected some of these as his own. At the age of ten he became a pickpocket. The reference to his beauty is no exaggeration. Throughout his long and varied career of crime he retained the handsome features and charming manners which characterized him as a boy, and were it not for the scars of knife and bullet wounds that are visible on his face he would now be a handsome man of striking appearance.

To-day there are scores of little half breeds playing about the streets and doorways of the Chinese quarter, but in the 60's the Appo boy was looked upon as one of the curiosities of the neighborhood, and among his playfellows in the Oliver Street School he was regarded as a sort of a juvenile hero, partly on account of his eastern ancestry and partly because of his nerve and cunning. He was a bright child, tricky and fearless, and as he grew into manhood he drifted naturally into one of the numerous gangs of roughs and loafers that were at that time so common in the lower wards.

As early as 1872 he was known as a James Street truck lifter—that is to say, he was in the habit of stealing tubs of butter and other commodities from the trucks that he found backed up against the sidewalk. "Nigger" Hannon, Archie Hadden, "Johnny" Foley and Dick Flannigan, known in criminal circles as "Dick the Tinker," were his associates in those days, and a choice crew they were, too. Young Hadden was the son of the notorious Hadden who kept a boarding house in Water Street where sailors were shanghaied every day in the week, and a near neighbor of his was a gentleman named Allen, who managed to acquire considerable notoriety at one time by posing as the "wickedest man in New York."

The young crooks who followed the learned profession of truck lifting along the river front undoubtedly learned a great deal from association with Mr. Hadden and his friend Mr. Allen, and for many years—until the police spoiled their usefulness—they were the terror of the neighborhood in which they lived and worked. One of their favorite places of rendezvous was a store or "fence" situated on Cherry Street, between Oliver and Catherine Streets, and kept by a woman named "Mag" Farley, the sister of the notorious "Red" Farley, better known in his day as "Reddy the Blacksmith."

It was here that George made the acquaintance of certain nimble fingered "ladies" and "gentlemen," who taught him the art of picking pockets, and in June, 1873, he was sent to the penitentiary for six months for practicing that art himself. When he came out of prison he adopted the light-finger business as a regular means of livelihood. About two years later he was again arrested for a similar offense, escaped from Bellevue Hospital, was re-arrested and sentenced to a second term, for he was now looked upon as an habitual criminal and a cunning, if not a dangerous man. His picture had its place in the Rogue's Gallery, and his face showing the characteristics of both his parents, was not a difficult one to remember and recognize—a circumstance which was a hindrance rather than a help to him in the profession which he had chosen to follow.

It is not strange that young Appo should have come naturally by a taste for opium smoking, a vice which held him enchained, and which has played an important part in his whole career of crime. As the Chinese colony grew in numbers, so did the opium dens within its limits increase and flourish; but it was not until late in the 80's that the passion for the drug began to spread among the Americans and Irish who dwelt in the neighborhood.

Appo had always, by virtue of his blood on his father's side, enjoyed to a certain extent the confidence of the Chinese—a confidence which these strange, secretive people seldom give to any one not of their own race.

While still very young he had learned to smoke and prepare the opium for the pipe, and it was through him that many New York roughs and crooks began to use the "dope" themselves and to spread the taste for it among their associates. They began to seek out the places in which smoking might be enjoyed, and in 1880, or thereabouts, there were a score of joints in full blast in Pell, Mott and Doyers Streets and in the lower Bowery, and not one of these but what had its quota of Caucasian smokers of both sexes, most of whom belonged to the criminal or dissolute classes. There were other visitors, too—actors, actresses, clubmen and those who dropped in from time to time for the fun of the thing and because they found a peculiar charm in the heavy, pungent, soothing atmosphere, and in the outspoken frankness and freedom which distinguished the conversation of the regular habitues.

At that time, the nice art of cooking or preparing the opium for the pipe was known to but very few except the Chinese, and the young halfbreed soon found that by means of his familiarity with the magical black paste and his undoubted skill in its preparation, life's pathway could be made smooth and delicious with a dreamy happiness, without the exercise of much industry or daring on his part.

There were a dozen ways in which he could pick up a living, if nothing more, through his connection with the joints, and any one of those ways was safer and easier than picking pockets or purloining things from trucks and basements. He could act as guide to parties of sight-seers who wanted to do Chinatown, and he could always earn a small fee and at the same time get his turn at the pipe by cooking the opium "pills" for the smokers who were less skillful than he. Besides this, continual contact with visitors from uptown offered him rather unusual opportunities for obtaining a watch or pin now and then without having to go to Benedict's for it.

So it happened that Appo became an habitual frequenter of the opium dens of Chinatown, and a "fiend" of the most pronounced description. That is to say, he soon became so addicted to the drug that he did not wish to exist without it, and it was probably on this account that when he was arrested in 1882 for the robbery of a Mexican named Del Valle, he made a desperate attempt to kill himself by drinking a vial of laudanum. On this occasion the Tomb's physician endeavored to adminster an emetic, but Appo kicked it out of his hands, and it became necessary to put him in a straight jacket and force the medicine down his throat.

The opium habit has always been a dominant influence in the career of this man, and it was through his indulgence in it that he came upon the great opportunity of his life, one which led to his leaving the business of picking pockets, which, after all, required only digital expertness and occasional fleetness of foot, and embarking in the beautiful green-goods profession, which called into play all the mental cunning and duplicity which he had inherited from his father, as well as the general "flyness" which came partly from his mother and partly from his long association with New York toughs, and in which he was an adept of the highest order and greatest proficiency..

Barney McGuire, at that time the acknowledged king of the green-goods men, was not only an habitual opium smoker himself, but was the proprietor of a joint of his own on Crosby Street, which was the favorite resort of some of the most agile artists in his line of busines. Barney and his craftsmen were not slow to recognize in Appo the qualities which have already been alluded to, and which they knew could be successfully applied to their peculiar calling. They said as much to him on more than one occasion, and it was not long before Appo began operations as a regular dealer in phantom counterfeit bills.

Now one of the strongest peculiarities of the opium habit is that when indulged in it stimulates the lying faculty to a degree that makes the exploits of Ananias seem trivial in comparison; and if there is any business in the world in which mendacity is at a premium it is that of luring yokels to the city and then making them believe they are going home with a package of bright new counterfeit bills in their possession. Mr. Appo's accomplishments in this line were such as would make him an invaluable salesman in an old furniture and rare bric-a-brac establishment, and in a very short time his talents began to waken the admiration of his fellows. It is not improbable that the business of awakening the cupidity of victims, drawing them to New York by means of a will o' the wisp green-goods letter, and then robbing them of their good money was one which appealed to the cynicism which is a part of the Eastern character, and is not altogether wanting in most professional criminals. For a time he prospered in his new calling, but it is recorded that in 1890, during a temporary depression in his peculiar trade, he so far forgot himself as to snatch a "yaller super" in a crowded downtown street, or in other words, to take a gold watch out of the pocket of a fellow citizen. For this he was sentenced to a year in prison. On his release he repented of his professional backsliding and renewed his correspondence with agriculturists in remote portions of the country. Up to this time George Appo had only been known to the police, to his own personal associates and to the occasional rustic who found himself in Jersey City with a black bag filled with a choice quality of fine hard-wood sawdust or a box of excellent tissue paper, for which he had paid the usual market price of about $125 a pound. The name Appo, it is true, had appeared in the newspapers from time to time in connection with some petty larceny or pocket picking exploit, but it was always coupled with the explanation that he was the son of Quimbo Appo.

George wanted to be famous, but fame came to him first in an unlooked for and wholly undesired manner, in the winter of 1893. It was early in February of that year that he went up to Poughkeepsie to meet an ancient and seedy "come-on" and his friend who had left their rural homes in the mountains of North Carolina, impelled by some alluring essays on the advantage of using counterfeit money, mailed to them by Mr. Appo, who had written them in a strain of imaginative beauty, such as can be found only in the "Arabian Nights." These "come-ons" wore long whiskers and had large rolls of good money secreted in their waistbands. They met their tempter in a room in a Poughkeepsie hotel, and the latter, finding his victims loath to part with their money, became threatening in his manner. He was promptly shot in the eye and the bullet went through his head. All hands were put under arrest, and Appo was removed to a hospital, where he again attempted to take his own life. It was thought at first that his wound would prove fatal to his reason, if not his life, but he recovered his senses in a day or so and was visited by a woman named Lena Miller, his common-law wife, and a gentleman who represented himself as a wealthy manufacturer from Block Island, a place which fairly teems with factories, as every summer visitor knows. His sweetheart wept when she saw the stricken crook, and the wealthy manufacturer inquired, with considerable anxiety, whether George had "given anything away." The wealthy manufacturer was none other than Walter McNally, brother of the notorious king of green-goods men, Jimmy McNally, now serving a term in state's prison in Illinois. Appo's nerves were in a horrible condition for want of opium, and he expressed himself with much bitterness in regard to his associate in the enterprise whom he referred to as "Dolph," and who, he declared, had sneaked off and left him to his fate. The Dolph referred to was Dolph Sanders, an associate and steerer for the notorious McNally green-goods gang. If it had not been for the influence of the Miller woman, who relieved his sufferings with small pellets of opium which she had brought with her, it is probable that he would have betrayed the members of the gang, as he claimed at the time it was a put-up job to do him. Three months later he got out of the hospital and was sentenced to a year's imprisonment. And sometime afterward, while being transferred from Sing Sing to Danamora in charge of Detective Jackson of Sing Sing prison, he again attempted suicide.

On his release he declared openly that the man who shot him was what was called a "dummy come-on," who had been hired by James McNally to put him out of the way, as McNally bore him a grudge. Appo said at the time that McNally and his professional associates bore him a grudge and employed this man to impersonate a rustic "gudgeon," and in that guise to kill him at the first opportunity. The game was considered a safe one, comparatively speaking, in view of the acquittal of the Texan, Holland, who killed the green-goods operator, Tom Davis, in New York City some years ago, and who was acquitted before Judge Roger Pryor. It was this suspicion on Appo's part, according to the testimony of some who know him, that led him to give away the operations of the gang at the Lexow investigation.

Such is the story of a man whose testimony regarding the mysterious workings of the green-goods business at that time proved a revelation to the entire country, and served as an amusing topic of conversation for the City of New York. As a study in heredity and racial traits and tendencies, George Appo's character is one which is well worth investigating, not only because of the way in which his peculiar talents have been applied to the business of money-getting, but also because he is the first one of the new hybrid brood to which he belonged who has come into popular notice. The question which naturally presents itself to the thinker is:

"What part will the rest of his tribe take in our national development?"

There is no doubt that many of the half-breeds will be heard of the same as was Appo. But it must be remembered that they are not all common, ignorant laundrymen and sailors, these pig-tailed aliens. Some of them are men of education, and even wealth, who have been brought up in their own native land as merchants or professional men, and there are many among them who would be termed, in Mr. Appo's picturesque lingo, "Fly mugs" (gamblers and sharpers), who surpass in cunning and mendacity the average confidence man of upper Broadway, and who journey from one city to the other playing faro as well as fan-tan, and fleecing those with whom they come in contact without regard to race or creed. Verily it is an interesting quarter of the town in which young men of the George Appo type are growing up, and we shall hear more from its half-breeds as time rolls on.

Appo had a hard time of it after his exploits as a Lexow witness. He was naturally hated and discarded by the green-goods fraternity, and was looked upon with suspicion by respectable people. Thus he became a veritable Ishmaelite, and experienced difficulty in getting bread to eat, either by honest industry or dishonest craft. He was hunted by his former associates, and was repeatedly in broils and fights with them. He was always under suspicion and frequently arrested. At last the state prison gave him shelter, from which he was removed to the Matteawan Asylum for the Criminal Insane, where he remains, a hopeless wreck like his father.

To attempt, according to the records of the much abused science of criminology, to trace a physical resemblance between father and son would be a superfluous task. Whether George Appo's insanity is the natural result of a career of vice and dissipation, or whether its seed was an inheritance long latent, is a question for alienists. The secret of his career is so simple that a child can see it. For George Appo to have led a pure and noble life would have required the moral strength of a Savanarolla, the genius of a Cromwell and the patience of a Job, qualities inconceivable in one man. For him to have lived as he did was—Human.

When George Appo gives up the ghost it will be the greatest benefit he ever conferred on his fellow man—more worthy of record than any or all of his long count of misdeeds. The approach of his death is in itself almost too trite a matter for comment. He has all his life been an enemy to all that is good and true in the world. He has done nothing but harm. He is so constituted that were he to be at liberty for a hundred years to come he would continue to do nothing but harm. In all fairness, such a man is better dead. But George Appo, insane, is another matter. With the loss of his reason he assumes a value that otherwise he could never have acquired. He teaches a wonderful lesson. If there is in all the world a human being who will profit by it, George Appo's appalling wickedness has not been in vain.

CHAPTER XXIX.

TYPICAL CHINESE.

BRIEF SKETCHES OF SOME OF THE REPRESENTATIVE RESIDENTS OF CHINATOWN, MALE AND FEMALE, YOUNG AND OLD, HONEST AND OTHERWISE.

HE foregoing sketch of the career of George Appo must not be accepted as typical of the Chinese colony in general. The good and the bad jointly make up that community, as the two classes compose all communities. The only true method of judging a body of people is to study all grades composing it. To aid in such study of Chinatown the following brief sketches of a number of its more conspicuous people is given.

CHU FONG—MERCHANT.

Chu Fong was born in Hong Kong, China, thirty-six years ago, and has been in this country nineteen years. Like the majority of his race he first came to San Francisco, there to learn the language and customs of Americans and the methods of trade between the two nations. After seven years' stay in San Francisco, Chu Fong came to New York, settling in the Chinese colony where he still remains. At present he is manager of the Hop Tai Wo Company, at 20½ Pell Street; also a large stockholder in the Choy Ding Quay Company, conducting the Chinese theater in Doyers Street, and a member of the Won Hing Company, Chinese importing and exporting house in Hong Kong.

Chu Fong is the son-in-law of Lee Chuk, a Chinese merchant of 21 Mott Street, who is said to be one of the wealthiest of his countrymen in the United States, various firms in which he is interested having branches in five of the large cities of this country and in Hong Kong, Shanghai and Canton, China. Lee Chuk also enjoys the proud and profitable distinction of being the Chinese Simpson, for by royal decree and permission he plies exclusively the trade of pawnbroker to the cities of his native land as named. Lee Chuk had a daughter, Sun Toy, who is the now proud Mrs. Chu Fong and the handsomest woman in the Celestial colony. Mrs. Chu Fong was born in Canton and is now 22 years of age and the mother of a young daughter something over a year old, whom her father calls Yok Ching Fong. The marriage of Chu Fong and Sun Toy afforded one of the most picturesque public ceremonies ever witnessed in New York. The nuptials were solemnized at the Lexington Avenue Opera House on the evening of October 21, 1892, by the Rev. On Nay, a Chinese minister, and besides 375 Caucasian guests who were present and at the feast which followed, there were 120 Chinese merchants, and the bride was attended by twelve Chinese bridesmaids. Many persons prominent in political, social and literary life participated in the function. Chu Fong has many friends in social and political life, numbering among them several ex-mayors, and others now and formerly high in official circles. Ex-Mayor Gilroy and Ex-Mayor Strong and Mrs. Strong have at different times enjoyed the hospitality of the Chu household. It was

MRS. CHU FONG.

Ex-Mayor Strong who formally opened the Mon Lay Won Restaurant, which is known as the Chinese Delmonico's, and it was Chu Fong, who, as a member of the Six Companies, the Four Brotherhood, and the Chinese

Merchants' Association, was chief of the committee of the leading Chinatown business men who tendered a dinner to Mayor Van Wyck and the new administration-elect at the Mon Lay Won on November 23, 1897—for which the most elaborate menu ever served within the boundaries of Chinatown was prepared.

Although Chu Fong is reckoned well-to-do, and was at the time of his marriage, he received from his father-in-law, Lee Chuk, who is an officer of the Six Companies, the unexpected but nevertheless substantial compliment of a dowry conferred upon Mrs. Chu amounting to $10,000 in gold. Mr. and Mrs. Chu Fong, aside from the immediate contact with their fellow country people, are somewhat Occidental in their tastes. Their home at 32 Mott Street is an ideal of what an American domestic establishment should be in all its appointments, and Chu Fong declares that his little daughter shall receive the best American education, befitting a woman, that American money can buy, and that his ambition is that she may live, and grow to that age when she may be able to teach and enlighten her frail sisters of the Orient in the language and ways of the "Mellican man."

JIN FUEY MOY—A CHINESE-AMERICAN DOCTOR.

Dr. Jin Fuey Moy, who besides being a practicing physician of the genuine American school, holds the position of official interpreter in the local courts, is perhaps the most happy exemplification of the highest attainment of polish and education, made possible for all his race in Free America. He came to this country in 1875, when but a boy of fourteen, to learn our language, embrace the Christian faith and become a missionary to his benighted fellows.

It was in Sien Ning, located in one of the four southern districts of the Kwong Tong Province of the Celestial Empire, that little Jin Fuey Moy was born. San Francisco was his first American destination, as it is usually for his fellow countrymen seeking these shores, where he remained but six months, and then came to New York.

DR. JIN FUEY MOY.

Soon after his arrival in the great metropolis several charitable and wealthy persons became interested in the youthful student, among them Mrs. George Washington Reed, of Brooklyn, and her husband (who was at one time publisher of the Brooklyn Daily Eagle), residing on Berkeley Place, that city.

In 1880 young Jin Fuey Moy became a pupil of the Pennington Seminary, Pennington, N. J., from which he graduated three years later. After his graduation he entered the Methodist Episcopal Chinese Mission at 14 Mott Street, conducted by the Methodist Episcopal Conference, as a missionary, where he remained until October, 1884, when he visited Philadelphia, where he took charge of the Chinese-American Union at 924 Walnut Street, a non-sectarian charity, covering a large field, over which Moy was made superintendent.

In 1886 he entered the Jefferson Medical College, Philadelphia, from which he graduated in 1890, taking the degree of M. D. He opened an office for the practice of his profession on Sansom Street, where he built up quite a large practice both among the Chinamen and Caucasians of the City of Brotherly Love. It was then that he Americanized his name to Jin Fuey Moy—Moy being his tribe or family name.

In 1892 he returned to New York and was associated for a brief period with Dr. J. C. Thoms, then conducting the Chinese Hospital on Hicks Street, Brooklyn, which was supported by voluntary contributions from various churches and private individuals. The hospital did not prove a success, and Dr. Moy severed his connection with it after having remained there but two months. After leaving the hospital Dr. Moy became superintendent of St. Bartholomew's Chinese Guild at St. Bartholomew's P. E. Church of this city, where he remained until January, 1897. He is now connected with the

District Attorney's office in New York City as official interpreter in the different branches of the criminal courts, a position to which he was appointed by former District Attorney Olcott, and reappointed by District Attorney Gardiner.

Dr. Moy still practices his profession among his fellow-countrymen in Chinatown, but says his patients are superstitious and are prejudiced against the scientific method of administering medicines, putting faith in various root and herb formulas handed down by bygone generations and to which they still cling with the simple faith of childhood.

Dr. Moy was married to an American lady in April, 1889, and is the father of a little daughter, now nine years of age. He resides at No. 18 West 134th Street, New York.

DEK FOON—BANKER.

Dek Foon was born in San Wing, Province of Canton, China, thirty-eight years ago. He came to America eighteen years ago, settling at Millsville, where he worked as a farmer for four months raising vegetables for the San Francisco markets. He then removed to Nevada City, where he opened a laundry, conducted it for eight months and then sold out at a profit. From there he came to New York and entered the employ of Wong I. Gong, as traveling salesman, collector and bookkeeper. He remained in the employ of Mr. Gong for eight years, when he opened a restaurant, and later entered into the advertising business at 24 Pell Street. He is also a partner in the Chinese banking firm of Joseph

M. Singleton & Co., at the same address. Dek Foon speaks and reads the English language fluently, although

DEK FOON—BANKER.

he never attended an English school, and is a self-made man. He is a Christian and one of the best known and most highly respected men in Chinatown.

CHIN YOU—MERCHANT AND THEATER MANAGER.

Chin You is a merchant, manager of the Chinese Theater, partner in the Mon Lay Won Restaurant, and managing partner of the Wing Chong On Company, 22 Pell Street. He was born in the town of Hok Son in the Province of Canton, China, thirty-one years ago. He has been a resident of the United States for fourteen years, the first five of which were spent in San Francisco,

CHIN YOU—IMPRESARIO.

where he served his business apprenticeship as clerk, bookkeeper, and manager of various Celestial commercial houses. At the conclusion of five years Chin You had accumulated sufficient money to allow of his return to his native land and birth place, where he wooed and wed Miss Leung Chin, whom he brought to this country, this time making New York his abode. On the second of March of this year (1898), Mrs. Chin You gave birth to a baby boy at their home, No. 32 Mott Street, a modern apartment house which is leased and sublet by her husband. Several of the wealthiest and most prominent of the merchants of Chinatown occupy apartments in this building, where they live in a style at once modern and comfortable.

SUE CHUNG CHEW—SPECULATOR.

One of the most intelligent and enterprising of the Chinese residents of this city is Sue Chung Chew. He was born in Sun Wai, Province of Kwong Tong, forty-two years ago. He is a full-blooded Chinaman, who migrated to the United States in 1869, taking up his residence in Oakland, Cal., opposite San Francisco. Being an enterprising young fellow he conceived the idea of acquiring a mastery of the English language, fully appreciating the advantage that would give him. By earnest work, steady application and determined perseverance, he had so far succeeded that in 1878 he was appointed interpreter in the United States Circuit and District Courts of California. In 1880 he lost a large sum of money, his own savings through industry and economy, in putting up a Chinese market building on Sacramento Street, San Francisco, He then removed to Portland, Ore., where he sought to recruit his fortune in the salmon canning industry on the Columbia River. He made some money at that, and then, in the fall of 1880, returned to China, and in 1881 married Miss Lumina Wang, also a full-blooded Chinese, though born in the West Indies. Sue Chung Chew started with his wife, March 28, 1882, to return to this country. They secured passage on a steamer of the Canadian Line, which was wrecked on Yesso Island, Japan, two weeks

SUE CHUNG CHEW AND HIS CHILDREN.

later. Chew lived among the Japanese for three months, finally, with his wife, securing passage to America, arriving for the second time on the first day of August, 1882. He remained in Portland a short time, where his first child, named Gertrude, was born. Then he removed with his family to this city. In the summer of 1887 he was employed on the Panama Canal, where he had the supervision and direction of the Chinese laborers. In

MRS. LUMINA CHEW.

the fall he returned to this city, and during the following winter traveled through the Eastern States delivering lectures on the religions of the Orient in churches and public halls. A second daughter, named Josephine, was born in Brooklyn, where the family was then living, and a son subsequently in Philadelphia.

Mrs. Lumina Chew was born in the Port of Spain, Trinidad Island, of a Chinese Christian family. Her father was Chinese interpreter at the English Court at that place. Miss Lumina, while yet a girl, was sent to Hong Kong to complete her education. She graduated from the Diocesan School in Hong Kong, and then became instructor in English to Lady Wu, the wife of the present minister to this country. She was born of Christian parents, reared in that faith, and died a Christian woman four years ago at Boston, Mass. The girls are now pursuing their studies in Hong Kong under private tutelage, but expect to return to this country to complete their education. The boy is now at Macao, China, studying.

CHIN SING—SCHOOL BOY.

This is an excellent photograph of a lad who is now a pupil in the public schools of this city, and a very bright and forward one. He can be seen any week day passing Paradise Park on his way to and from school. His name is Chin Sing. He is the son of Chin Yee, who is quite a prominent man in Chinatown, residing with his family at No. 12 Pell Street. The father made a small fortune in smuggling bogus Chinese merchants into the country from China, defying the proscription. He bought a little small-footed woman for his wife, paying $1,000 for her. He wants to buy another, and says he will do so just as soon as he can lay his eyes on one that suits him. Chin Yee is considered wealthy and highly respectable in Chinatown, of which he is one of the leading citizens.

CHIN SING—SCHOOL BOY.

MRS. THOM JOCK—A "NEW" WOMAN.

Mrs. Thom Jock is the wife of a cigar manufacturer of Howard Street. She was born in China and came to the United States for the purpose of studying the English language. While so doing her money gave out, and she had to struggle for a living. Mr. Thom was in New York at the time, but was thinking seriously of going to China to buy a wife. He did start and got as far on his journey as San Francisco. There he met this lady, and quickly became enamored of her. Within a few hours, and by the expenditure of a few hundred dollars

MRS. THOM JOCK AND CHILDREN.

to her relatives, she became Mrs. Thom. One of her sons is named Thom Wing Jew, and is a public school student. When he puts on his Sunday clothes in American style, he looks to be the cleanest little Chinaman that ever walked Pell Street. Mrs. Jock is deservedly proud of him.

MRS. MON LEE—A CHINESE MOTHER.

Mrs. Mon Lee is a well preserved woman about 32 years of age. She was born in China, but married in this city about ten years ago. She lives with her family

MRS. MON LEE AND CHILD.

at 21 Mott Street. Mrs. Lee is the mother of a bright three-year-old boy, and a girl six years old. Her husband, Mon Lee, is a naturalized citizen of the United States, but has never been allowed to vote. He is a pig roaster and sausage manufacturer by trade. He is about 50 years old, and wears eye glasses and a mustache.

MON NGEE—MISSIONARY.

Mr. Mon Ngee is a Christianized Chinaman, now serving as a missionary among his own people under the

MON NGEE—MISSIONARY.

auspices of the Young Men's Christian Association. He is now traveling in the northeastern portion of New York State, expounding the truths of Christianity to his fellow countrymen. Mr. Mon Ngee is about 31 years old. He was born in Hock Shan, Province of Kwong

Tong, and came to America ten years ago. He acquired his education in the Sunday Schools and by private study. He is said to be the brightest bible scholar among the Chinese converts in this country.

LUK POR—A MONEY-MAKING WOMAN.

Luk Por may not be this woman's name, but it is the appellation by which she is generally known. It is the

MADAME LUK POR.

Chinese equivalent for Grandma. Luk Por is an old slave, who lived in California thirty years before coming to this coast. Here she has been a member of Wo Kee's family, at 19 Mott Street. During her lifetime she has succeeded in saving $12,000, which is a large fortune for a Chinese woman. Of course she no longer has any value as a chattel, and being free to go and come as she pleases, purposes to return to her native land and spend the rest of her days there, which she can do comfortably on her fortune. She is still active and able to maintain herself by her labor. Besides serving the Wo Kee family, for which she is accorded a home and board, she finds outside employment in combing and dressing hair, running errands, and serving as a midwife. She is also a Ching Ching Joss and inspires luck for other Chinese ladies. For such services she is paid handsomely. She has grown-up sons and daughters living in China, to whom she frequently sends money. Through her aid the children are now prosperous and considered highly distinguished in the district where they live.

DANG FEY—A FAT MAN.

The next picture speaks for itself. It is a portrait of Dang Fey, who lives at 19 Pell Street, and who has two recommendations to notice. He is the fattest Chinaman in town, tipping the scales at 310 pounds. Moreover he is a wonderful sleeper. He frequently sleeps two and even three days at a time. He is compelled to sleep alone, notwithstanding that he is a married man. This is because of the perpetual motion he maintains while asleep. He rolls from one side of the bed to the other continually while sleeping. Should he roll upon his wife he would inevitably crush her. The fear of such a misadventure compels them to use separate beds. You may see him sit at his desk to dispose of some business, but within three minutes he will be fast asleep in his chair and snoring musically. It is said that despite his somnolency Dang Fey eats as much as any three ordinary Chinamen.

DANG FEY—THE FAT MAN.

CHU JIN—A YOUNG MERCHANT.

Chu Jin is a young man, a member of the Lun Chun Company, of No. 4 Doyers Street. He is frequently employed as interpreter in the courts, and is the youngest interpreter in the city. He married an educated Chinese lady of his own age and choice last winter. His father promises him all the backing he may require to carry on his business enterprises. He is a Christian, nevertheless is highly respected by his fellow Chinese who yet cling to heathenism.

CHU JIN—A YOUNG MERCHANT.

LEM TONG SING—A PROMINENT HIGHBINDER.

Lem Tong Sing, alias Charley Tong Sing, alias Scar Face Charley, is the head man of the Hip Sing Tong. The police say he is one of the most notorious cutthroats ever known in Chinatown, and it is alleged that he is responsible for five or six murders that have been instigated by the highbinders in the United States. He is always closely watched when he is in the jurisdiction of the Sixth Precinct. Sing is a remarkable man in many ways. When he first appeared in Chinatown, early in 1882, his countrymen of the clique opposed to the Hip Sing Tong became terror stricken, and some of them asked the police for protection. "Scar Face Charley" is the name by which he is best known. After his fourth week of residence in New York he made application to the police board for appointment as special detective in Chinatown. He said that gambling was going on constantly in nearly a score of places and that the regular police was not able to suppress it. He has a scar about five inches long across his face. He claims he received the injury while in the Arctic regions. He was at one time steward on the steamer "Jeanette," and later on the "Thetis," in the Arctic regions. He has two medals, one presented by Congress to the survivors of the "Jeanette" expedition, and the other presented by the Navy Department.

Quan Yick Nam, a Chinaman who has done service for the police of the Sixth Precinct, became the object for attack of the highbinders, and the price of $1,000 was said to be the reward for his death. Nam, who had been in San Francisco when Charley Sing was there, gave Police Captain Young the whole story of Charley's career of crime. Nam says that Sing killed a man and got his papers, and has since passed himself off as the original

CHARLEY TONG SING—"SCAR-FACED CHARLEY."

owner of the papers. Ex-Assistant District Attorney George Gordon Battle said that Sing has something of a record in Newark, N. J. Twelve years ago he and several confederates tied up and nearly killed a countryman of theirs. For that Sing served a long term in state's prison. His next escapade consisted of a bold daylight robbery at the store of Willie Hong, in Fair Street, Newark, N. J., on November 10, 1895. Sing and four confederates attacked Hong and took $101 from him. Sing and another Chinaman named Wing Sing, were arrested red-handed, but their companions escaped. Members of the Hip Sing Tong offered to repay all the money taken if Willie Hong would not prosecute, and when that offer was rejected, threats were used. The two Chinamen were tried in Newark and they set up the plea that they had been playing fan-tan in Willie Hong's place and had been arrested for demanding their winnings. A gullible jury believed the story and acquitted the prisoners. The term served by Charley Tong Sing in Trenton State's Prison was ten years for burglary and highway robbery.

LEE SHEW—POLITICIAN.

Lee Shew is considered the most powerful politician in Chinatown. He is the leader of the Lee family in the Eastern States, which numbers about 3,000. He is an enterprising merchant, the proprietor of two large stores in New York and one in Boston. He is a member of the firm of Sang Chung, 24 Mott Street, and Sun Chung Lung, 3 Oxford Street, Boston. Lee Shew is about sixty years of age. He is a cousin of Tom Lee, a former Mayor of Chinatown.

YAN PHOU LEE—SCHOLAR AND WRITER.

One of the bright men of New York's Chinatown is Yan Phou Lee, a graduate of the Class of '87 at

Yale College, and consequently a particularly bright individual.

Mr. Lee first visited the United States in 1873, when he was 12 years old, as one of the 120 Chinese sent out under the auspices of Li Hung Chang to obtain an American education. He went through the grammar school,

YAN PHOU LEE—SCHOLAR.

the preparatory school for colleges, and entered Yale in 1880. In 1881 the Chinese Government recalled all its students, and Mr. Lee returned and was assigned to the Tientsin Naval Academy, but afterwards resigned, as he did not consider himself fitted for a position in the navy. In 1884 he returned to Yale and was graduated with high honors in 1887.

Mr. Lee had not the money with which to pay for his college course, and to repay the amount he entered the lecture field and traveled from New England to the Everglades of Florida, telling American audiences of "Chinese Customs and Manners." By this he earned sufficient money to keep him and pay the debt he had contracted.

During the Chinese agitation on the Pacific coast Mr. Lee became a contributor to various magazines on the subject of discrimination against the Chinese, one article from his pen, under the caption "The Chinese Must Stay," in the North American Review attracting considerable attention.

After he was through his lecture course Mr. Lee embarked in the mercantile business in a town near Wilmington, N. C., but at the end of two years went to San Francisco and was given a position in the Pacific Bank, controled by the McDonalds, who were his classmates in Yale. He remained there eighteen months and then returned to New York, and for three years past has been Chinese interpreter in the courts here.

When Li Hung Chang arrived in the metropolis Mr. Lee was engaged by the New York World to accompany the Viceroy during his stay and write up the various functions attended by him. During the time the gentleman in Yellow Jacket was in poor health, and refused to be interviewed by the reporters. But being known to him the Viceroy gave Mr. Lee an advantage over the others by according him an audience three days before an edict was issued allowing reporters to enter his presence. Mr. Lee paid a visit to his home two years ago in relation to a concession granted him by the managers of the Tennessee Exhibition, which took place in 1896 in Nashville. At the request of the management he brought to the United States the material for a building of a typical home of a Chinese agriculturist. In addition to this he also brought a Chinese family, so that visitors to the exposition could see how the Chinese live. This was done by an act passed by Congress at the time permitting the Chinese to enter the United States for the purpose of attending the exhibition in connection with a concession.

Mr. Lee's home in China is in Hong Shan, or "Fragrant Hills," just north of Macao. He knows of Mr. Afong's place there, and knew Tony and Chun Lung when they were students at Hartford and New Haven respectively. In 1887 Mr. Lee wrote a book entitled "When I Was a Boy in China," and was fortunate enough to sell the copyright to the Lothrops in Boston for a good round sum. The money earned in this venture enabled him to travel extensively in the United States, and he has visited nearly every city of importance in the country.

After he graduated Mr. Lee declared his intention to become a citizen of the United States, and renounced his allegiance to the Emperor of China. During his visit to China it was as a citizen of his adopted country.

APPENDIX.

VIEWS OF VARIOUS PROFESSIONAL WRITERS AND OTHERS ON CHINATOWN AND THE CHINESE QUESTION.

CONTENTS.

Lucien Adkins—"A General View"............ 295
Wm. E. S. Fales, Ex-Consul at Amoy........... 298
Elbert Rappleye—"Chinese Humanity"......... 302
Wm. W. Young—"Chinese Peculiarities" 307
Isaac D. White—"Among the Vicious"......... 312
Horatio Jennings Ward—"Sight-Seeing"........ 316
Edward E. Pidgeon—"Sunday School Work".... 319
Police Inspector Brooks—"General Characteristics" 323

EXPERT OPINIONS.

VARIOUS VIEWS OF LIFE AND CHARACTER IN CHINATOWN BY THOSE WHO HAVE MADE STUDY FOR YEARS—DIFFERING VIEWS FROM DIFFERENT STANDPOINTS.

I have endeavored to give a plain, fair and impartial portraiture of Chinatown and those who inhabit it. Nothing has been written through prejudice or favor, nor has any effort been made to color the features that make this locality so peculiar. Lest this should be charged, the views and testimony of those best qualified to judge Mongolian character, habits and pursuits, because of their intimacy with them, have been secured at great pains. Prominent writers on the metropolitan press who have made Chinatown a specialty in their news gathering have furnished me with signed articles illustrative of their experiences, which are printed herewith as received. Hon. William E. S. Fales, former United States Consul at Amoy, and himself a trained journalist, also contributes an interesting sketch, placing Chinese and American morals and habits in striking juxtaposition. Police Inspector Brooks, who has been brought into close official contact with these strange people, also contributes a valuable paper, telling of the efforts made to suppress vice in that quarter. From these various sources a comprehensive and perfectly impartial estimate can be formed of New York's Chinatown as it actually is to-day.

LUCIEN ADKINS—A GENERAL VIEW.

Not many years ago an unfamiliar might sit in a Chinese restaurant until he starved. If he did not know what to order, he could get no suggestion from the Chinamen. They preferred to cater to their own people. They distrusted the Caucasian. Their attitude was not odd. They were strangers in a strange land, and the whites with whom they came in contact were, usually, of the lowest kind. By comparison, in their estimation the Chinaman was a superior person in every way, and it is no wonder that he became an egotist and held in contempt a race so manifestly inferior.

Within recent years the conditions have changed. The armor of Chinatown has been penetrated. Curiosity and research have led many well-bred and considerate men and women into the Oriental colony, and the result has been a better understanding on both sides. The Chinaman, quick to grasp business advantages, has seen the possibilities of trade growing out of the interest he was free to excite in the American mind. He now does business with all comers, and he does it with fairness and ability.

In the Chinese restaurants of to-day you will be given a bill of fare, with the names of the dishes printed phonetically in English, and if you are in doubt as to what to order, the Chinamen will take a great deal of trouble to put you right, and will bring samples of half a dozen dishes.

As a friend and guide, I have introduced many to the delights of chop-suey, a standard dish that stands the test of time much as does the roast beef of old England. It can be eaten once every day, and it is a wonder how the desire for it manifests itself in the man who lives principally on French cookery.

Take a friend to Chinatown for the first time and watch his face when the savory chop-suey arrives. He looks suspiciously at the mixture. He is certain it has rats in it, for the popular superstition that the Chinese eat rats is in-bred. He remembers his schoolboy history, with the picture of a Chinaman carrying around a cage of rats for sale.

He quickly puts aside the chop sticks, which are evidently possessed of the devil, and goes at the stuff with a fork. It is a heroic effort, but it is not sustained. The novice gets a mouthful or two, turns pale, all the time declaring that it is "great."

It is a long time before he can be persuaded to go again, but he is sure to surrender eventually to the enchanting decoction, and soon there are times when the knawing hunger for chop-suey, and for nothing else, draws him to dingy Chinatown, alone and solitary, if he can find no one to accompany him. For awhile he half believes there must be "dope" in the stuff. He is now certain that there are no rats in it. He is a confirmed chop-suey eater.

There is much to interest the thoughtful in the Chinese colony. To know the Chinaman is to like him; to find that, despite his race, his religion, his Oriental traditions so far from everything European or American, he thinks just as we do, has the same notions of pride, of honor, of justice and of morals, and can readily be made into an acceptable American citizen.

Admitting that at first he is a semi-barbarian, he is impressionable, clever, shrewd, and, above all, most honorable in his dealings. It is marvelous how quick he grasps the new and how well he retains the old impressions. Personally, I would extend the right hand of friendship and citizenship to the Chinese people. It is not possible in the allotted space to tell why.

Lucien Atkins.

WM. E. S. FALES, EX-CONSUL AT AMOY.

There are two Chinatowns. That of odoriferous and queer restaurants, gaudy joss houses, pretty shops and busy stores is well known to Gothamites. There is a second which is known to but few Americans. It is the

Chinatown of benevolent societies, of clubs and unions, of social relations and of home life.

All tradesmen are more or less alike. A Chinese shopkeeper is like his Western colleague, the chief difference being that the Oriental sells goods at a lesser profit. Restaurants vary but little the world over; soup and stew, roast and boiled, cake and pastry, sweetmeats and preserves, entree and hors d'oeuvre, tea and wine make up the Mongolian as well as the Caucasian bill of fare. The former is older than the latter and has therefore a greater variety of foods and dishes. Religions are cast in the same mould. The Buddhist and Taoist believe in God, immortality, the punishment of wrong, the reward of virtue, the power of prayer, the efficiency of faith, the forgiveness of sins, the action in this life of spiritual forces, both good and evil, a day of judgment, a heaven, a hell and many of them in a resurrection of the body. They are nearer orthodoxy than many Christian churches.

Those who study Chinatown are at first bewildered by the color and glitter; after that they find that everything is just like its counterpart in "Little Italy," the "New Jerusalem," or the "Swedish Colony."

But the other Chinatown is a world full of novelties. In it are born the co-operative banks, institutions by which a poor man of good character can raise $50, $100 or even $1,000. Here are benevolent societies and charitable funds. Some support the sick, bury the dead, provide for widows and orphans, or carry remains from New York to family burying grounds under the shadow of the White Cloud Hills in distant Canton. Others bring skilled physicians across a continent or help enterprises in Cuba, Porto Rico or Panama. Others aid the unfortunate or keep the prayer house in repair. Insurance and assurance, co-operative and profit sharing, the loan and building fund association, the mutual benefit society, the corporation limited, the syndicate, trust and pool, the labor union, employers' union, arbitration board and other features of the best part of American civilization appear here in similar or in more developed forms.

Here are circles of six or a dozen who, after their work is over, sit or recline listening, while one of their number reads aloud the poems, essays, stories, and histories of their literature. Here you can have related to you the dramatic tales of the wars of Canton with the armies of the North; the marvelous accounts of Tamerlane, Zenghis Khan and Kubla Khan, who conquered and ruled over more territory than Alexander, Caesar Augustus, Charlemagne, Mahmond, Charles V. or Napoleon Bonaparte; or the magnificent lives of Foo and San Tszoon.

Here are poetic competitions, in which cook and waiter, salesman and laundryman, gambler and merchant appear as rival bards producing verses so smooth and sweet as to seem the pencraft of professional writers.

Here, when you are known and liked by the Chinaman who has been made taciturn, moody and suspicious by hoodlumism and cruelty, you can hear the hopes and ambitions, the life comedies, tragedies and romances of the little almond-eyed commonwealth.

Here Wing Sing gave a great dinner when he won the prize in a contest. The conditions of the tournament were severe. Each candidate was required to submit a verse four lines long with eight words to each line, the first word of the first line to be "dragon," and the last word of the last line "ship." In English his poem would run:

"Dragon, who rules the shoreless sea of death,
When I lie dreaming on my loved one's lip
And thou dost come to take her parting breath,
Oh, take me with her on thy spectral ship."

Here Ah Fong reads every evening from 8 to 12 in Yuet Sing's private office the romantic history of the warrior Wong Tai, who saved the empire from the heathen of the North.

Here Yuet Sing received his pretty little wife from Canton and held open house a fortnight to express his joy. Here died the last of the Hwangs, the Taeping generals who would have overthrown China but for Chinese Gordon and his British and American free lances. Here passed away Ting Hop, who was tried and convicted of stealing the burial and charity funds of one of the Tongs, and who took opium to avert a more awful fate. This is the true Chinatown, one which once seen will never be forgotten.

Wm. E S Fales

ELBERT RAPPLEYE—CHINESE HUMANITY.

The bravest man I ever knew was not a Chinaman; but one of the strangest acts of bravery I ever witnessed was performed by a Chinaman.

I never knew the names of any of the individuals who figured in the incident, which began in Hope, a little railroad town in northern Idaho, and ended in a building in Pell Street, just off Mott. I happened to see the beginning and end of this story while covering assignments for the New York Mail and Express.

In Idaho, as in all the West, there are more Chinese women in proportion to the Chinese population than in the East, and although the possession of a wife, negotiated in the usual manner, is about as expensive a luxury as in New York State (less the cost of transportation), there are more wives; more women; more female associations; and it is in consequence of that, perhaps, that the women out there are more human than the torpid, apathetic, calloused victims of licentiousness who are exhibited in New York's Chinatown to the gaze of the alien as "a Chinese woman."

One of these Western women of her race was the wife of a merchant in Hope. He was wealthy—I was told. She was good looking—I was told; but I never saw her. I heard about her jewels and her attendants, and I gathered that they were plentiful. Her husband, or at least her owner, was a very striking figure. He was of ordinary stature, but erect. He had fine features, which indicated a degree of intelligence unusual for a Chinaman. His voice was pleasant—which was more remarkable. He was altogether a figure, noting which one would naturally inquire about, and having done so myself, his identity was established as I have described it —a wealthy merchant. My informant added: "He is more like a white man than a Chinaman. He is a sport, gambles like a gentleman, loses like a sucker and will go broke without a holler," which in Hope, Idaho, at that time described a thoroughly worthy citizen.

I became fairly acquainted with him during the two weeks I was there, and found out that he furnished labor to the railroad and gambled against his luck, and, what struck me as a trifle peculiar, because of the primitive ideas I had of the domestic affairs of the Chinese, he seemed to think considerable of his wife.

About two years later I was covering an assignment which took me into New York Chinatown to see Captain McCullagh. I was walking through Mott Street when I came face to face upon a Chinaman whom I recognized as the figure impressed upon my memory in Hope. I hailed him, and he greeted me, but without spirit; and while I was mentally measuring his changed appearance and calculating how long it was since he had "gone broke without a holler," I asked him why and when he came here.

"Lose all money. No luck. Mebbe year flom Hope. Much tlouble."

I got the story straight finally. The miserable wretch had sold his wife. "Her heap cly," he said, and he persuaded me that he felt bad, too. It had been a year since he had seen her, although she was here in Chinatown, the wife of some other Chinaman.

Suddenly our conversation was interrupted by a cry, which to me was unintelligible, and a frantic Chinaman came tumbling out of the hallway of a tenement a few doors up Pell Street. Both of us hurried to the point, and by the time we reached it there was an uproar in every direction, and then the voices of women screaming: "Foh-sheu!" (Fire!) as they came tumbling out of the hallway after the Chinaman. Then Chinamen, white women, young ones and nondescripts followed until it seemed as if the population of several such tenements had emptied itself on the street. I recollected later that I did not see any Chinese women among the wildly excited fugitives. In another moment the hallway was filled with smoke, and it rolled out of the cellar and first-story windows in a suffocating cloud. Then the faces of some Chinese women appeared at some of the windows above.

We were standing watching, my Chinese acquaintance exhibiting no excitement, until among the faces of the Chinese women he recognized some one, and pointing upwards he shouted something in Chinese and then darted across the street into the smoke and disappeared in the hallway.

By this time the rattle of approaching fire engines, and the shrieks and moans of the scores who had turned out from the human bee hives in the neighborhood, together with the hollering and excitement, made such a scene as it is possible to witness only when the cry of "fire" is heard in one of the dense tenement districts of the great city. I had not ceased to wonder for a moment what had become of the Chinaman, and was looking for him when he suddenly appeared again, dragging out through the smoke a Chinese woman. The crowd hurried around them, and I could understand that the woman was endeavoring to break away and get back into the house. In another moment, however, I saw her rescuer plunge back into the smoke, which was now so dense that it meant almost certain death to anyone attempting it.

Then the firemen broke in, and in another moment the crowd was scattered. More fire bells were clanging and the police were hurrying to the scene, and driving the people out while the hose was being dragged in. But while all these scenes, typical of a New York fire, were taking place, I was peering anxiously for a glimpse of the Chinaman who had gone back through the smoke in response to the appeal the woman had made. I watched until the fire was subdued, but I saw nothing of the life-saver. It was only a cellar blaze, and as the smoke quickly lifted the firemen could make their way into the halls without difficulty. They had just done so when two of them came out dragging a body.

"One of the Chinks," I overheard a fireman say, as I recognized the limp form of my friend; indeed, I felt at that moment as though I might be proud to have had such a friend. As the firemen were laying a blanket over his body another came out of the door bearing in his arms a little child wrapped in a bed quilt, and they had found it near the body of the man who had tried to save it.

It was perhaps two weeks subsequently when I was in Chinatown again, and although I do not believe in ghosts, I was almost frozen by coming face to face with that identical Chinaman. I must have shown it. I stopped in amazement; perhaps it was a feeling of terror. I don't know which; but he came up to me, held out his hand and I believe I shook it in a manner which described my perplexity, for he smiled broadly and said:

"Me no dead; too muchee smoke. All lite now."

"Well, I thought it was all over with you," I said; "but what has become of the woman? Was she yours?"

"She my gall—Hope."

"And the baby that I thought you had died for—?"

"Not mine—hers."

Elvert Rappleye

WM. W. YOUNG—CHINESE PECULIARITIES.

"Foh Sheu! Foh Sheu! Foh Sheu!"

A thousand terror stricken Chinamen repeated the cry, running wildly up and down Mott Street and through the narrow lanes dignified with the names of Pell and Doyers Streets.

"Foh Sheu! Foh Sheu!" echoed a thousand other Celestials, as they rushed to the second, third, fourth and fifth-story tenement windows which line the street like dark entrances to cliff swallows' homes.

"Foh Sheu! Foh Sheu!" shrieked forty timid little almond-eyed women from the land of tea, temples and toms-toms and their rich silk skirts rustled as they shrank into the dingy corners of their dark rooms.

All was confusion. Bedlam was turned loose. One might imagine that he had been suddenly dropped among the frantic people of Pompei as they fled from lava-belching Vesuvius.

There was a three-alarm fire in Chinatown, and I was sent by the New York World to "cover" it. It was midnight, early in winter, 1894, and it was my first reportorial assignment in that queerest of all foreign colonies in New York. The burning building was one of the densely populated Chinese tenements in Mott Street.

Blazes are the bane of Chinamen. They fear flames as they do death. Whether the fire be big or little the excitement in the narrow streets is intense. Alarms spread more rapidly there than in any other section of the city, for no other section is so thickly peopled and the people nowhere else are so closely joined by common interest or so watchful of each others safety.

At the first shrill cry of "Foh Sheu! Foh Sheu!" which means "Fire! Fire!" a host of sleepy Celestial souls spring from their "lay-out" bunks; thousands of almond-eyed, yellow men swarm out of the dark, narrow doorways, like rats in buildings fleeing from danger, carrying with them their most precious belongings. Chattering and gesticulating wildly they rush aimlessly about the streets.

This happened to be an uncommonly fierce fire, and the commotion was proportionately great, so my introduction to New York's Chinatown was lively and interesting.

What I saw that night made me want to see more—a natural result of any American's first visit, I believe, even under the most commonplace circumstances. I have seen much more, greatly to my advantage professionally, and infinitely to my personal satisfaction.

From the burning building that night forty-six scantily clad Chinamen escaped through a single rear window, dropping to an adjoining roof. To be sure, there was a suspicious rattling of coins, which indicated that the inevitable fan-tan had centralized the population for the time being. While these panic-stricken yellow men clambered out of that window, hundreds of others hurried through numerous other windows and through the single front door. One Chinaman attempted to escape through a fourth-story window. Hanging by his fingers on the sill he could just touch the top of the third-story window frame with the toes of his bare feet. Reaching adjoining buildings was impossible; to drop would mean death. So, although the fire gradually crept toward him, there was nothing left for the frightened man to do but hang on for dear life until some fireman climbed a ladder and came to his rescue. This was done, but the frightened Chinaman remained in that perilous position, suspended high in the air, fully ten minutes before assistance came.

The thought comes to me that these two incidents of my first Chinatown fire, the escape of the forty-six Chinamen through a single window, and the pluck displayed by the suspended man, were good illustrations of two very important characteristics of the Chinese—concentration of population and tenacity.

A Chinaman is nothing if not tenacious. He will hang on to anything, from a peculiarity to a principle; he will stick with equal tenacity to a fact or to a falsehood. Arguing with him is of little use. No other people are so completely controlled by custom as they. For a thing to be customary makes it right in their eyes, even if it is wrong.

The houses of Chinatown are like huge honeycombs, but only drones occupy them. Inside them are many labyrinthian lanes, lined with dark and dingy cell-like rooms, rickety stairs running from sub-cellars to roof.

Most Americans who visit Chinatown see only the surface. They have no idea of the conditions existing behind the walls of the buildings there. Under some of the buildings there are as many as six sub-cellars, each occupied by Chinamen as a living apartment or as a dark, vermin-reeking hiding place for their opium "lay-outs."

I was once sent by the World with a photographer to get photographs of a Chinese woman connected with the Chinese Theater in Doyers Street. At the theater they told me she lived in a Chinese lodging house in Chatham Square. I went there and was told by an excited crowd of Celestials who caught sight of the camera that she did not live there. Chinamen hate cameras.

After spending an hour trying to locate the woman I went back to the same building, feeling sure that she really did live there. My experience had taught me that the best way to deal with Chinamen is to show them that you are not afraid of them. I was getting angry. Leaving the photographer behind, I started on an exploring trip through the house alone, opening the door to each room and looking for the woman. On the fifth floor I found a temporary bridge leading from the fire-escape to the fire-escape on the next house back. Not having found the woman I crossed this bridge and began searching the next house, calling the woman's name in each room.

Down, down, I went, floor after floor, until I thought the house had no bottom. At last I found the woman, and, upon making an investigation, found that we were in the fourth sub-cellar under the Chinese Theatre. I had gone through a doorway in Chatham Square, and when I again emerged into daylight it was from a door leading into Doyers Street. By a great deal of persuasion I got the woman to put on her most gorgeous gown and climb over fire-escape and all, clear to the roof of the Chatham Square house, where we made photographs of her.

Chinatown is a fertile and fascinating field for reportorial work. Fact or fancy may form the writer's theme, and the result will assuredly be interesting if the Chinatown flavor is retained. The colony is a news mine that may be, and is, successfully worked by observing writers. There are nuggets of news to be picked up daily; there are nuggets in the shape of special articles for the Sunday papers and the magazines in every building in the place, in every phase of its commercial and social life and in every one of its curious customs.

Wm. W. Young.

ISAAC D. WHITE—AMONG THE VICIOUS.

I am afraid that I am not very popular in Chinatown, due to the fact that for three or four years I took part in nearly all the raids made by the police on the opium dens and fan-tan games, and on a few occasions attended government officers in their search for smuggled opium. The Chinamen naturally enough learned to associate me with their misfortunes, for whenever a raid is made there are many arrests and everything pertaining to the violation of law is confiscated. The spoil includes opium, pipes, lamps, yen-hocks, hop-toys, fan-tan checks and any loose money that may be found on the gaming tables.

When Police Inspector Nicholas Brooks, then a captain, took command of the Sixth Precinct, which includes Chinatown, the law regarding opium smoking and fan-tan was violated almost openly, and he made up his mind to clear the atmosphere. His wardmen, who were also new in the precinct, were Frank Price and John Shirmer. They spent their spare time for several weeks locating the dens, and learned, among other things, that they were best patronized on Sunday nights, when Chinamen from surrounding towns come to New York to spend a holiday. Accordingly the first raid was planned for a Sunday night.

All the reserves were kept in the station house that evening. Not one of them knew what was in the wind, for news spreads quickly in Chinatown, and if the slightest rumor had been sent abroad there would have been no more smoking or gambling for a good many hours to come. About 10 o'clock I set out with Captain Brooks, Gustav Roeder, another reporter, two wardmen and a trio of policemen in citizen's clothes. We sauntered into Mott Street in pairs, keeping well apart. Price and Shirmer were in the lead, and when they ascended a flight of steps a few doors from the Joss House the rest of us promptly followed. Once indoors we made a rush up a couple of flights of stairs, burst open the door and found ourselves inside of one of the biggest "joints" that Chinatown supported.

A person who has once been inside an opium joint will

never forget the smell. The close, fetid atmosphere was clouded with smoke, and the pungent odor of the poppy permeated everything. There were thirty odd Chinamen and three American girls packed away in a couple of rooms that would have made comfortable sleeping apartments for not more than three ordinary beings. They were laid out in groups of two or three in little low bunks, arranged one above the other in a double tier that extended all around both rooms. Each group had the regulation lamp, a pipe and a "shell of dope." A few slept, but most of them were smoking.

There was a rush for the windows when we broke in, but we were too quick for the Chinamen, many of whom seemed very "dopey" indeed. When they realized that they were properly coraled they became sullen and silent. A couple of policemen were left on guard, and the rest of us hastened to the next den that had been marked by the detectives—hastened because we wanted to arrive there before word got abroad that the police were on the rampage that night. Two other opium joints and a fan-tan shop were surprised in the next half hour and the inmates placed under guard.

Then word was sent to the station house for the reserves, and upon their arrival the prisoners were marched off in pairs. A wagon load of smoking and gambling paraphernalia was confiscated, including ivory-tipped pipes beautifully colored, with orange peel bowls and silver "saddles;" hop-toys graven with dragons and mystic figures; little brass lamps with delicately tinted globes and trays or salvers of wood and metal, curiously decorated. A majority of the "lay-outs" were much more common, however, than those described.

In the biggest raid I ever attended in Chinatown we

took, I think, ninety-eight prisoners. As an illustration of the docility of the Chinaman, I recollect that three of us that night were left alone in a "joint" with forty-eight prisoners, and not one of them so much as moved to escape pending the arrival of the reserves.

A few days after this raid I went with Louis J. Beck to dine in the restaurant under the Joss House. I recognized in the waiter one of the former prisoners, and from the conversation which followed I was forced to conclude that he remembered me.

"What want?" he asked sharply.

"Two chow-chop-suey," I replied.

"No Sabee; no chow-chop-suey," said the Chinaman, sullenly.

"Then dong-gow-gi?" I requested.

"No dong-gow-gi," was the prompt response.

"Well, what have you got?" I asked, impatiently.

"All the samee no allee," he said, and he marched away from the table with much show of dignity. We had to go elsewhere for our dinner that night.

Isaac D. White.

HORATIO JENNINGS WARD—SIGHT-SEEING.

The funniest combination I've met with since I became a newspaper reporter was General Booth-Tucker and Steve Brodie. The place was Chinatown.

Brodie had invited the General to come down to the Bowery and see the sights, and incidentally he invited a number of newspaper men to come around and see "the fun." Nobody ever goes slumming in the Bowery without taking in Mott Street and its crooked tributaries, and there was no exception in this case. The whole thing looked like a put up job. When the General arrived at Brodie's place at 10 o'clock that night Steve was there to meet him.

"Walk in, General; I see you're on time," was Steve's greeting. "Come in an' I'll fix yer fer de trip."

Steve then took the General into a room in the back of his saloon and adorned the classical features of the leader of the Salvationists with a pair of huge false whiskers and a wig similar to that worn by "Svengali." They then started on the now famous "slumming trip."

Mike Callahan's saloon was the first place visited. There the General had to pay $2.50 for a round of drinks, and in getting his change had a bad quarter "worked off" on him. This Steve kept as a memento. The next place was the Joss House in Mott Street, with the Chinese restaurant below. There the General had his pockets stuffed with gifts of chop sticks, pastry and tea. A cup of the latter was brewed for him, but he seemed afraid to drink it. The Chinese temple interested him hugely. Particularly the sacred drum. The General could not keep his hands off it. Twice he hit it a resounding whack to the horror of the attendant. He would certainly have been thrown out by the "Chinks" had it not been for Brodie, who pacified them by distributing some silver dollars, which the General produced.

In the Joss House the whiskers of the commander of the Salvation Army attracted universal attention. The ladies of Chinatown were particularly pleased with them. The General was well satisfied with his disguise, however, and never dreamed that the denizens of the dives were "onto him." He had just left the temple loaded down with incense sticks and other relics when a policeman stepped up to him and said:

"Don't you know you are violating the law?"

"I don't understand," said the General. "What am I doing?"

"The 'gazaboes,' " said the policeman, giving the false beard a twig. "You'll have to come around to the station house," continued the officer, as he took the General by the arm.

Booth-Tucker was horrified.

"Dis ain't on the square," said Steve. "De General is me guest and he ain't bein' treated on de level, see."

"Well, you ought to know," answered the policeman, as he gave Steve a wink.

The General was arraigned at the station-house desk, searched and detained in the back room, while Brodie signed away one of his brown-stone houses as security for the General's appearance in court the next morning. Of course Steve was profuse in his apologies to the General for the treatment he had received.

"I meant no harm," said the General when he appeared in court the next day with the notorious Steve by his side. "I wanted to meet the sinners that I was sure Mr. Brodie could bring me into contact with, so I put on the whiskers, as I did not want to attract attention." A few days later when I met Steve he said:

"How's dat for a story? I'm goin' to pull off anoder in a few days, and I'll put yer on, see."

Horatio Jennings Ward.

EDWARD E. PIDGEON—SUNDAY SCHOOL WORK.

My first opportunity to study John Chinaman beyond the sidewalk observances of boyhood, disclosing him as a human clothes sprinkler, was in the class room of a Brooklyn Sunday School, where a number of Celestials attended each Sabbath.

To my young and untutored mind this gathering of silken-bloused attendants comprised the most demurely modest and devout followers of the faith it had ever been my juvenile privilege to observe.

Their apparent eagerness to throw off the blighting shackles of heathenism and embrace the teachings of the new Christ were beatific in the extreme, and these Orientals, some of whom had not only renounced the creed of their forefathers but the queue and habiliments as well, were pointed out as great and glorious examples of the good and mighty result of the evangelizing influence of missionary work here, and its needs in far away heathen climes.

For a time only one or two churches in elite neighborhoods were the proud possessors of Chinese classes, who in all the gorgeousness of their best raiment, added not a little spectacular color to the picture of the Sabbath afternoon gatherings, while certain it was, the missionary interest did not suffer abatement nor did the contributions for the foreign missions diminish.

A few years later I found myself one of a band of earnest young workers who volunteered their services to teach the Celestial attendants at the Chinese Mission of the Methodist Episcopal Church (the first of its kind established), in the very heart of Chinatown.

There I found the same intelligent, perceptive and ready pupil of the Sunday School, who would, even with only a smattering of our language, learn in the brief sessions of two successive Sabbaths the entire alphabet—and remember it. I recall two such brilliant scholars.

The new mission was a novelty that did not fail to interest even the denizens of that populous and then exceedingly wicked quarter, and the attendance increased steadily until it was impossible even to accommodate more or procure sufficient teachers for those enrolled, for it required a tutor for nearly every scholar in the early stages of their educational development.

My apt pupils soon reversed the conditions, and I then began to learn something myself. For a time the attendance was most regular. No sooner, however, had we become interested in and justly proud of the remarkable progress of some favorite scholar who had mastered the primary intricacies of the "three R's," than the familiar face was missed from the Sabbath gatherings. Gradually one by one they would, with few exceptions, silently and unannounced drift away from the Christianizing influence of the mission, and—as we afterwards learned—out into the world to battle with their fellows for Uncle Sam's gold, that commands so high a premium in the Chinaman's native land.

The laureate of Poker Flats hath spoken truly. The reason was plain. Each had in a few weeks of patient application, with the honest aid of a few earnest souls, equipped himself with what, in his limited sphere of usefulness was all sufficient for the great mercenary struggle in the big Metropolis. Chinamen, except in a few isolated cases, do not depend on their race for their money-getting, and the wily Celestial having received from his philanthropic Caucasian brother the necessary means for business intercourse and incidental financial emolument, is, as a rule, satisfied to consign the future salvation of his soul to indefinite postponement.

Many years of newspaper labor, which have necessitated hundreds of visits to Chinatown and contact with its people, have but confirmed the long-lingering suspicion that the Semites are not the only race who possess the commercial instinct uppermost. The moral is plain.

John Chinaman, as we have learned to familiarly call

him, is a thrifty and naturally domestic individual, of a stolid, suspicious, secretive disposition, a man of few enjoyments, industrious and honest in business affairs, and to those endeared to him, generous to a fault. Religion—the Christian religion—is usually to him an easy and ready means of launching him on a straight course of prosperity, and then—well, nine hundred and ninety-nine out of a thousand of these aliens live in the hope of accumulating here a sufficient competency to enable them to return to the Flowery Kingdom and pass the remainder of their days in comfort and the worship of their favorite Joss. There is little or no humor in his composition, although one will occasionally meet one of the Christianized stamp who has sufficiently absorbed our civilization to appreciate a jest of the mildest order, and it was such who christened the writer one sweltering summer day as he mopped the perspiration from his heated brow—"Su-Bock-Up"—which in the patois of the Cantonese means "Boiled Pigeon."

Ed E. Pidgeon

POLICE INSPECTOR BROOKS.

POLICE INSPECTOR BROOKS.

GENERAL CHARACTERISTICS OF CHINATOWN—THE PREVALENCE OF VICE AND CRIME, AND EFFORTS TO SUPPRESS IT—WORK OF THE POLICE IN THE LOCALITY.

There are about 1,500 Chinamen living within the Chinatown district, of whom about 50 are married. On Sundays and Mondays this number is increased to about 3,000, the cause of the increase being that relatives and countrymen from the surrounding cities visit the locality for the purpose of business, smoking opium, gaming or visiting the Joss House.

Of the married Chinamen about one-half have native (Chinese) consorts. There are about 50 children in this district of whom about one-half are descendants of native parents. All the children are sent to the public schools.

The Chinamen of this district do not deviate from their original customs but adhere strictly to the Confucian rites. They also wear their native dress, very few of them having adopted European ideas or clothes.

The Chinamen in general are thrifty. Those interested in commercial pursuits are a better class. Their principal occupations are laundrymen, keepers of small stores, such as groceries, laundry supplies, medicines, Chinese herbs, dealers in general merchandise, teas, silks, curios, etc., cigarmakers, barbers, tailors, and a few carpenters. There are about 15 Chinamen, each employing three or four hands, engaged in agricultural pursuits on Long Island. Their principal stock is vegetables raised from seed brought here from China. They bring the product of their farms to Chinatown where they dispose of it. Gin-seng, a herb which grows in large quantities in this country, is largely exported to China. There are about four or five firms exporting gin-seng. One firm claims to have exported $150,000 worth of it during the past year. It is worth about $8 a pound. Ginseng is supposed to have qualities for renewing lost vigor. Chinese shoes and material for their dress are imported, the Chinese tailors making up the material to conform to the Chinese style.

The principal points of interest in Chinatown are the Joss House, at 16 Mott Street; the Chinese Theater, at 7 Doyers Street; Chinese restaurants, at 11 and 16 Mott Street, and 22 Pell Street; Chinese Masonic Hall, at 4 Mott Street; the Mission, at 17 Doyers Street; Chinese printing office, at 3 Doyers Street, and the offices of the Chinese Six Companies, in the rear of the Joss House. Barber shops are also worth visiting here.

The Joss House consists of one large public place of worship, a portion of which is sub-divided into small Joss Houses, one for each clan or family. Small Joss Houses are visited as frequently as the majority of us attend our churches. Upon each visit an offering of food or other material is given to Joss. The large Joss House is used on holidays. The Chinamen has only one holy day and about twenty holidays. The holidays are principally births of statesmen, etc. Their only holy day is their New Year's day, which comes sometime between January and April. On this day every Chinaman, no matter how sinful or immoral he may be, visits the Joss House, burns incense and appeals to Joss, who gives him a ticket which reveals his fortune for the ensuing year. They have elaborate and extensive celebrations lasting for about two weeks. During this period the Chinaman does no more work than is absolutely necessary to supply him with food. No banking or other work is done.

The Chinese Theater is opened daily from 6 P. M. until midnight. The prices of admission vary with the time that you visit the theater, viz: if you enter at 6 P. M., you pay 50 cents; at 8 P. M., you pay 35 cents; at 10 P. M., 25 cents, and at any time after that, 15 cents. The play generally lasts from six weeks to six months.

The restaurants are patronized principally by Chinamen. Slummers drop in occasionally to see the natives eating their food with their chop sticks, and generally order a native dish so as to be able to say they ate in a Chinese restaurant.

The Mission in Doyers Street for the conversion of Chinamen to the Christian faith and for their instruction in the same is conducted by Americans. Occasionally a Chinese convert will relate his experience or hold the services.

The printing office at 3 Doyers is now used principally for the printing of laundry tickets. A weekly Chinese paper was issued from this place, but through lack of subscribers and advertisers it was forced out of existence.

The office of the Chinese Six Companies is visited by

every Chinaman before he begins speculating or starting in business of any character. Their visit is principally for advice, or to get an endorsement from the company which gives them as much commercial standing as a rating in Bradstreet's or Dun's would give to one of our firms.

The Mayor of Chinatown is elected and takes office on their New Year's day. He holds office for one year. His principal occupation is to settle disputes, etc., no lawyers being allowed in Chinatown.

There are no surgeons in this district and the only medical practitioners are herb doctors. In almost every case of sickness, whether from a headache, broken arm or leg, fracture of the skull, or any other sickness or injury, a decoction of herbs and reptiles (lizards, snake skins and mud turtles being principally used) is administered to the patient.

The business firms are of a co-operative nature. All of the stockholders who are employed in the business receive a salary. At the end of the year the balance is divided equally among the shareholders. Many of the large firms are at present upheld with the money from the small laundrymen, who, in addition to the profits derived from their laundry, get a dividend yearly from these establishments.

Vice and crime is prevalent in Chinatown to a degree that astonishes Americans. This is largely due to the different notions of morality the Chinese hold from those of Christian nations. With them gambling is not considered wrong, nor is the promiscuous intercourse of the sexes. They are largely addicted to opium smoking, which may be said to be a national vice.

I was appointed to command the Sixth Precinct,

which includes Chinatown, on January 24, 1891. At that time the locality was overrun with gambling dens and opium joints, and I determined that, so far as it lay in my power, I would drive them out. Accordingly I instructed my wardmen to procure all the evidence they could against the principal dens of iniquity, and on the sixth of February I made my first raid on a gambling den at 24 Mott Street, where we captured twenty-four prisoners.

On March 17, I again made a raid, this time on an opium joint at 104 Park Street, where eighteen men and women were arrested and a number of opium layouts and quantities of opium were confiscated. On April 21 I raided the dens at 6, 10 and 12 Doyers Street and 13 Pell Street, where I captured 40 men and women. After this raid the Chinese got together and formed an association which they called the "Fan-tan Players' Association." It was formed with the express purpose of warning the gambling dens of the approach of the police, but was not successful in its object.

I received complaint on June 24 that there was a young girl 15 years of age in a den at 11 Pell Street who was being outraged by the Chinamen. Accordingly on the 26th I raided the place and rescued the girl from her awful position and made a number of arrests.

The Chinese were by this time in a frenzy of fear on account of my raids, and whenever a policeman put in an appearance in citizen's clothes the cry would go up: "Mock-a-hi!" which means "Lookout for the police!" Despite all they could do, though, I continued to raid their joints, and on August 5 I raided the joints at 32 Pell and 13 Mott Streets, and captured thirty-six Chinamen, twenty layouts and some money. At both these places there were watchers on the outlook for the police, but we fooled them by getting behind trucks and making a sudden dash into the place. When we entered the joints the frenzied Chinamen made an effort to put out the lights, but my men were too quick for them. They then made a dash for the windows, and some of them escaped, but were afterwards found hiding in a closet in the back yard and taken to the station.

On September 7, I raided the opium joint at 6 Doyers Street and arrested forty men and women. On September 27 I raided the den at 104 Park Street, where I rescued a little girl who was held prisoner by the Chinamen. When my men appeared with the prisoners the crowd went wild on learning that the little girl had been held in the den. They threw stones at the Chinese prisoners, and some one threw a lasso at one of them, but it landed on a policeman.

The biggest raid I ever made was on November 8, when I captured ninety-one prisoners, a large number of opium layouts and a big copper boiler full of opium. The places raided were at 105 Park Street and the basement and second floor of 21 Pell Street.

During the fifteen months I had command of the precinct I continued my raids and when I left the place was pretty well cleaned out.

Nicholas Brooks
Inspector

MOSES H. GROSSMAN.

Mr. Moses H. Grossman, an American attorney, of the law firm of Friend, House & Grossman, has played no small nor unimportant part in the business affairs of Chinatown. He has searched and passed upon the titles to almost every inch of ground in the Chinese locality, as counsel for many of the heaviest property holders. As a result he has made himself thoroughly conversant with Chinatown, and has, upon many occasions, escorted select circles of visiting friends through the streets and alleys and into the temples and apartment houses of that interesting quarter. He is universally popular, and so well liked by the denizens of Chinatown, that his visits, which though now quite infrequent, are ever welcome, and those who have the good fortune to visit Mott and its adjoining streets under his able guidance, never want for interest or enjoyment. Mr. Grossman was formerly a newspaper man, and as such originally made the acquaintance of the then Mayor of Chinatown and his conferees. When he was graduated from college he was the valedictorian of his class, and when he was admitted to the bar, the esteem and respect of many of the Chinese officials and property holders, compelled them to entrust him with the management of their property and legal affairs.

www.ingramcontent.com/pod-product-compliance
Lightning Source LLC
LaVergne TN
LVHW010538100826
845148LV00001B/229